DECORATIVE SOLDERING

For Stained Glass, Jewelry, and Other Crafts

by Trudy Thomas

Aurora Publications
6214 Meridian Avenue
San Jose, CA 95120
(408) 997-0437

ISBN 0-913417-00-9

Table of Contents

To Mom, who taught me never to say "I can't."

Decorative Soldering - The Final Touch

1

For those of us who have worked with copper foil, soldering the seams has always been a tedious and uncreative step. We have strived to emulate the smooth, rounded and uniform appearance of lead came. The only creative decisions to be made at this point were the width of the seams and the color of the patina. Stained glass is a highly decorative and expressive art form and deserves more than a simple bead. We now offer a way to make the soldering as expressive and creative a part of stained glass as the glass selection and subject matter itself. The solder no longer has to be just "the thing that holds the glass together". We call this new technique DECORATIVE SOLDERING.

Decorative soldering is the artistic application and manipulation of solder. It requires the use of special flux, solder, and tools.

This technique is applicable to all forms of stained glass, both flat work and structural projects. The technique is also useful in other forms of arts and crafts, such as jewelry and sculpture. The finished appearance of a flat window can be greatly enhanced with the careful application of decorative soldering to all or portions of the window. The beadwork that is decorated has a tendency to stand out. Therefore, it is an excellent way to emphasize the focal points of your work. The texture you choose can either blend with or complement the subject matter of the window panel. For example, if you are doing a natural scene with a bird standing on a fallen tree along a creek bed, each of these three main items can be accented with complementary decorative textures. The seams of the bird can be finished in a wispy texture resembling the edges of feathers. The soldering of the tree area can take on the rough texture of bark. You can even add some free-form vinework on or around the seams. The rocks along the creek bed can be accented with textures resembling sand and/or pebbles.

The possibilities are unlimited. You can now feel free to be expressive and creative when you solder. All my students agree that they can now make even the simplest window panel a work of art.

The application of decorative soldering to structural projects enables the artist to greatly enhance the appearance of the simplest box or planter. Decorative accents can also be added to more complicated structures; such as lamps and free-form sculptures. I have found that a simple jewlery box becomes an elegant piece of art with the addition of decorative solder beadwork that sparkles from the light of the lamp. A vase cap that has been decorated is a beautiful way to accent a stained glass lamp. The lighting fixture can also be decorated with solder to add an even more individualized artistic touch.

One of the biggest questions most people have about this technique concerns the amount of time involved. For the professional craftsperson, there is always the question of cost efficiency. Will the extra time devoted to creating a decorative bead be adequately compensated for by an increase in the selling price? The answer is an unqualified YES.

The hobbyist, as well as the professional, will attain a higher degree of satisfaction from this creative new technique. Pride in one's work is always important to the craftsperson. With practice, you will soon find that it often takes less time to achieve a highly decorative bead than a perfect "came-like" smooth bead. The inability to achieve a uniform smooth bead has often been the downfall of an otherwise good craftsperson.

The information contained in this book is designed to give you all that is necessary to get you started in this new and exciting technique. We will give you detailed information on the best tools and materials to use in achieving the various decorative soldering textures. We will also give you ideas for various special applications such as decorated vase caps, lighting fixtures, jewelry, belt buckles, free-form sculpture, etc. Information is included on mounting jewels or stones on your projects and on making decorative wire hangers for small window panels. We also discuss ways to prepare various surfaces for soldering.

We will give you step-by-step instructions, including illustrations, of all of our most popular textures. We will also explain how to combine certain textures for additional variations. Tips will be included to help determine what textures to use for certain applications, such as texturing edges and corners, and "bridging" or building with solder.

Also covered are recommendations for special cleaning, polishing, and patining techniques of your decorative solder, which eliminates, some difficulties that may arise with the highs and lows created in many of the textures.

All we can teach you is the foundation of this exciting new art form. Most people find that they quickly begin to develop new textures through experimentation. Many supposed "errors", if repeated, can become a new texture. There basically are no failures, just new discoveries.

2 Tools and Materials

During the years that we have been doing decorative soldering we have tested many different tools and materials to find what works best. The recommendations that we make may seem quite extensive but they all have very definite purposes. We will elaborate as we go along.

Soldering Irons

The selection of the iron or irons that you use is critical. We recommend using a lightweight, well-balanced iron with various interchangeable tips, or several irons with different tip sizes. The Ungar #7760 handle has proved to be the one that fits the specifications most closely. A 40 to 45 watt iron seems to work best, as this gives you the maximum power and heat necessary for some projects. The tips should be rated at about 1000 degrees. This temperature varies with manufacturers. The tips that we most frequently use with the heater are chisel style in three sizes; 1/8″ (Ungar #PL - 113) or (Ungar #PL - 151), 3/16″ (Ungar #PL - 133) or (Ungar #PL - 153), and 1/4″ tip comes on Iron Assemblys 1140A (40 watt) and 1145A (45 watt). These tips can be screwed onto a 1000 degree heater (Ungar #4037-S). The Ungar 1/4″ tip and heater #4037-S can be substituted by heater-tip combination #4033-S.

We recommend that you use three separate irons in your work as it is quite time-consuming to change tips during work on your project. The use of a few different irons enables you to maintain good speed and rhythm. Frequent texture changes and resulting necessary changing of tips on one iron can become quite a bother during a project.

We like using a lightweight iron because many of the textures require a delicate and rhythmic touch that is more easily achieved with a lightweight iron. Heavy-tipped and large-bodied irons are harder to control and make it difficult to maintain consistency of texture. They also are too tip-heavy to easily achieve very delicate textures. A detailed explanation of the various uses of these tips will be given in this chapter, as well as in the individual texture instructions.

Generally speaking, the 1/4″ tip is used for assembling the structure, tinning all seams, laying down any preliminary beadwork under the textures, and for some texture work done on large heat-absorbing surfaces, i.e., vase caps, belt buckles, and large solder-filled spaces. Certain textures are also best executed under certain conditions with a 1/4" tip. These will be explained in later chapters. The 3/16" tip is used to achieve larger texture patterns on areas that do not absorb too much heat. The 1/8" tip is used to achieve most of the finely detailed textures on most standard bead widths. The 1/8" tip is also a must when working on jewelry and some free-form sculpture.

Rheostat or Temperature Control Unit

It is essential to be able to control the heat of the iron's tip to achieve most of the textures described in this book. Textures with more detail usually require a cooler temperature as well as a smaller tip. When texturing is done on larger, heat-absorbing, surface a higher temperature is required. That same texture done on a narrow bead will require a cooler iron. The detailed instructions for various textures included in this book will give ideal temperature settings for each texture and some possible variations.

Flux

Flux is an agent that cleans and prepares a metal surface for soldering. The most important thing to remember in selecting a flux is that it should ideally burn clean and wash away easily. It is essential for it to burn clean in order to see the texture created as you are working it. The residue left by some fluxes can impair the view of your work. This residue is often quite difficult to clean from the low spots in your texture and can often adversely affect the patina and polishing of the finished piece.

Solder

We recommend using solder of the highest quality (Canfield makes a high-quality solder in the three types that we use.). Low-quality solders contain impurities which, when burned, create inconsistencies in the texture and can leave crusty residues which are quite undesirable.

Solder is a combination of tin and lead. The higher the tin content, the greater the detail that can be achieved. Since tin is harder and cools more quickly than lead, it allows more detail to remain in the solder as it cools. The higher the lead content, the longer the solder will remain molten. Thus, it has a greater tendency to smooth out as you work it.

We mainly use three types of solder: 50/50 (50% lead / 50% tin) used for the basic assembly of the piece, tinning of seams, standard smooth beads, and basic low beads required under textures.

60/40 (60% tin / 40% lead) is also recommended for smooth beading and for many of the more defined textures on larger surfaces. It is basically the best all-around solder as it can, with practice, be used for all aspects.

63/37 (63% tin / 37% lead) can be used for delicate textures where you want very highly defined detail. This is also a very versatile solder, which we refer to as "super solder" because of its ease of use and purity. "Bridging" or building up of solder, is most easily achieved with solders that have a high tin content.

All the other tools and materials used are standard stained glass tools and materials. One thing to consider is that you might want to use a wider foil in areas to be textured. This will give you a larger area to achieve the desired textures. Wider seams are no longer an undesirable feature when decorative soldering has been applied. THE SEAMS NOW BECOME AN IMPORTANT PART OF THE ARTWORK.

Textures 3

On the following pages you will find detailed, step by step instructions on executing our most popular textures. In Chapter 5 you will also find instructions on modifying and combining these textures to create even more textures.

These textures are combined into basic categories: (1) BACKGROUND (can be used alone or in combination with another); (2) HIGHLIGHTS (applied to a background texture or solid bead to create emphasis); and (3) WHOLE BEAD textures (these textures cover the entire bead and are not generally used as backgrounds or highlights). These categories are only general, and you may find exceptions as you use decorative soldering more frequently.

Before beginning to practice these textures, we recommend that you make a type of glass "notebook." This is a cluster of glass strips upon which you can practice, experiment with, and compare your textures. Cut 12 (or more) one-inch strips of glass (clear window glass is fine) to a length of 10 inches each. We recommend foiling them with 1/4" foil as this will give you a nice wide bead upon which to practice your technique. In future projects you may also want to use a wide foil to enable you to execute a well-defined detail. Very narrow foil often does not give you enough room to properly define your texture. You can experiment with this in the future.

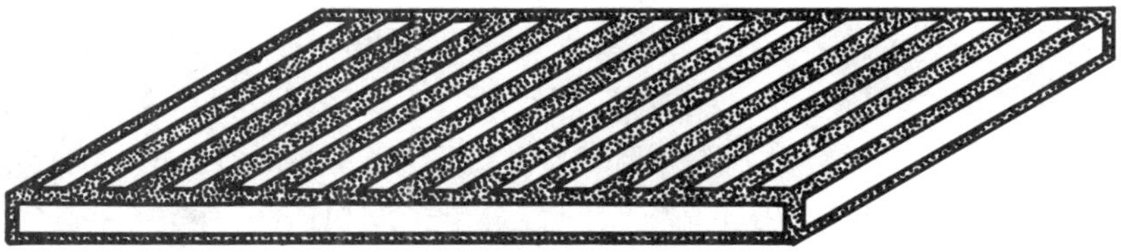

FIG. 3-A....Working Practice Notebook

Tack the foiled strips together to form your notebook (see fig. 3-A). Sides can also be added, upon which you can practice edge and corner textures. When working on your notebook you may want to erase used areas by simply melting away the solder.

The individual texture instructions will include recommendations for the type of base solder bead upon which to work. We will describe them here rather than repeat them in the individual instructions. TIN ONLY means that the foiled surface be coated only with solder; no buildup is necessary. FLAT BEAD requires that all gaps be filled and a low thin bead of solder be applied; about 1/32" thick is sufficient. BASIC BEAD is as it sounds; it should be the same smooth bead that you would ordinarily use as a finished bead on your project. Fig. 3-B shows an end view of all three of the above beads.

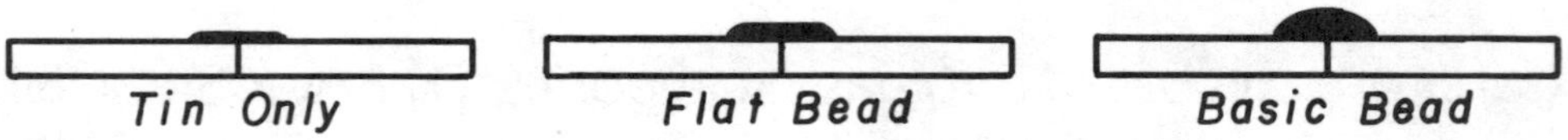

FIG. 3-B....Base Solder Bead

SOLDER comes in three different alloy combinations. The instructions will recommend either 50/50, 60/40, or 63/37. The recommendations are based on which solder is easiest to use to achieve a desired texture. With experience you can modify your procedures to use other solders in some circumstances.

TIP WIDTHS will be recommended for the finished texture; either 1/8", 3/16", or 1/4" will be called for. The 1/4" tip is always recommended for laying any type of base solder bead. These tip width recommendations are based on the idea of working on a seam that is approximately 5/16" wide (1/4" foil on single-strength glass). With experience you will find that the tip width necessary to execute a certain texture may vary with the size of the area to be soldered. See Chapter 5 on Variations for further details.

TEMPERATURE CONTROL SETTINGS are given for the recommended tip size and type of solder. You will have to vary the settings if you do not follow the tip size and solder recommendations given in the individual texture instructions. The size of the bead or area to be textured will also affect the temperature settings (cooler for small areas, hotter for large areas). This will also be explained in Chapter 5.

The temperature control settings are based on my equipment and may vary depending on the soldering iron and type of rheostat that you are using. You should be able to compensate for your equipment by adjusting the settings up or down about 10%. You will quickly find your range and be able to adjust all recommendations.

On certain textures SPECIAL RECOMMENDATIONS may be given to help you with the texture.

WHEN BEGINNING A NEW TEXTURE BE SURE TO THOROUGHLY READ ALL INSTRUCTIONS, PAYING SPECIAL ATTENTION TO THE ANGLE AT WHICH YOU SHOULD HOLD YOUR IRON.

BE PATIENT—SOME TEXTURES WILL TAKE QUITE A BIT OF PRACTICE TO PERFECT.

4 Texture Instructions

BE SURE TO READ ALL INSTRUCTIONS AND THE SECTION ON HELPFUL HINTS BEFORE ATTEMPTING TO DO A PARTICULAR TEXTURE. BE SURE YOU KNOW AND UNDERSTAND THE ANGLE AT WHICH TO HOLD YOUR SOLDERING IRON. BE SURE TO PAY SPECIAL ATTENTION TO WHERE TO APPLY THE SOLDER ON THE BASIC BEAD.

BEGIN A TEXTURE BY FOLLOWING ALL RECOMMENDATIONS GIVEN AT THE BEGINNING OF THE INSTRUCTIONS. THEY ARE DESIGNED TO GIVE YOU THE BEST CHANCE TO ACHIEVE A "PERFECT" TEXTURE AS SOON AS POSSIBLE. WITH TIME AND EXPERIENCE YOU WILL BE ABLE TO MODIFY THE RECOMMENDATIONS TO SUIT YOUR OWN STYLE AND NEEDS.

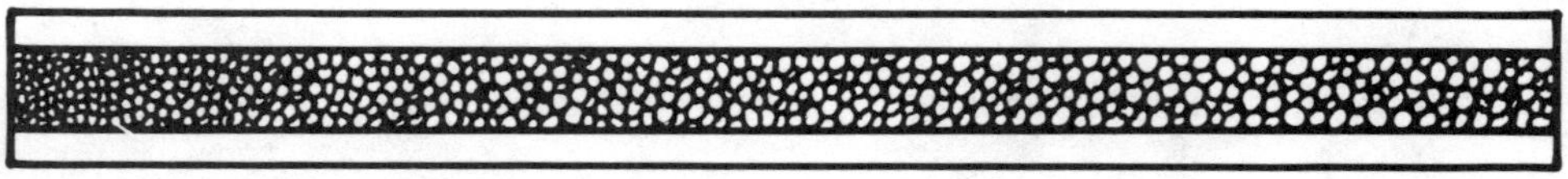

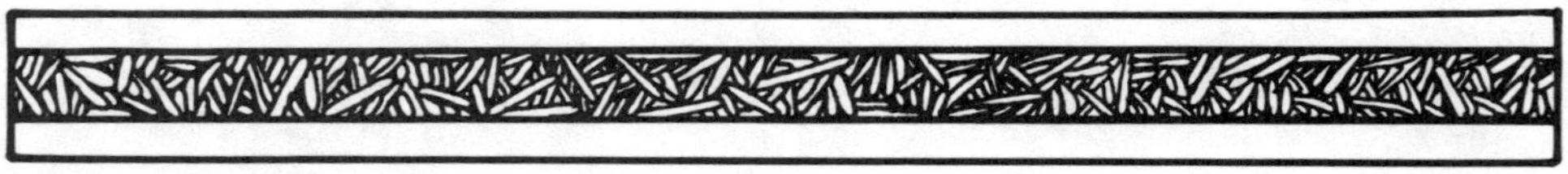

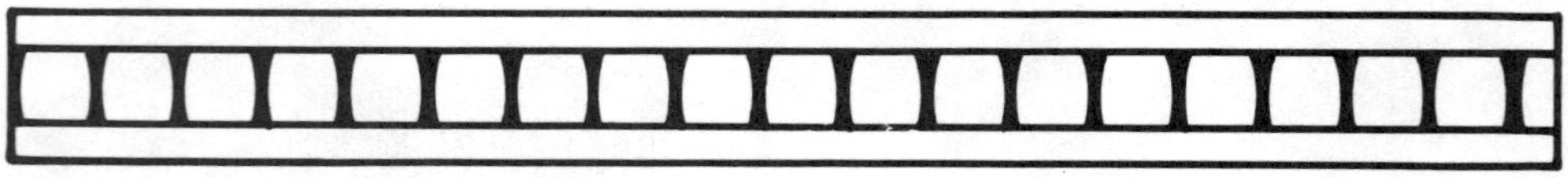

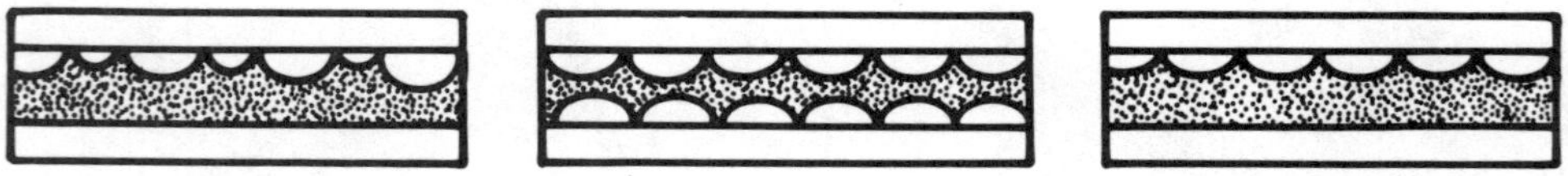

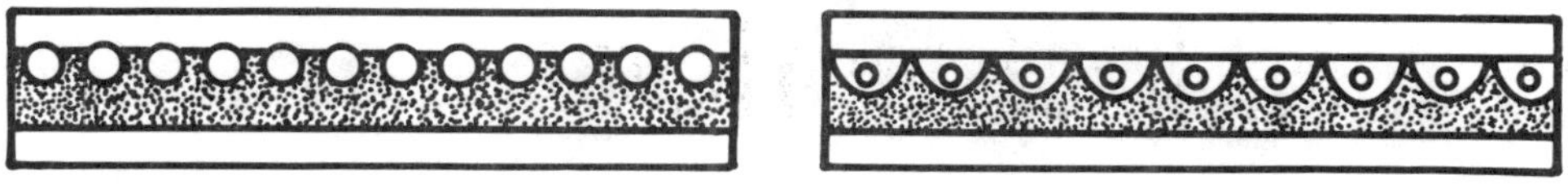

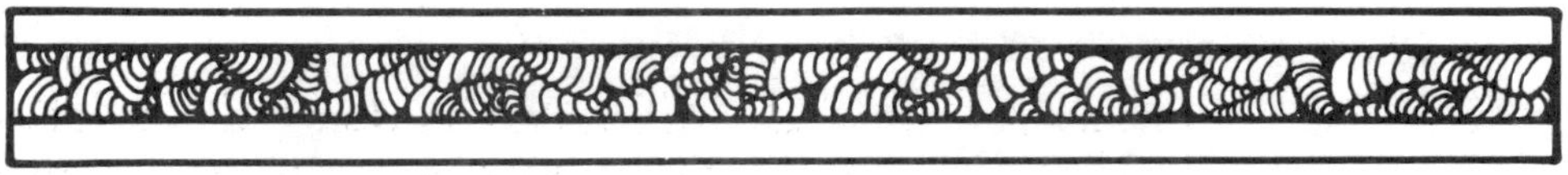

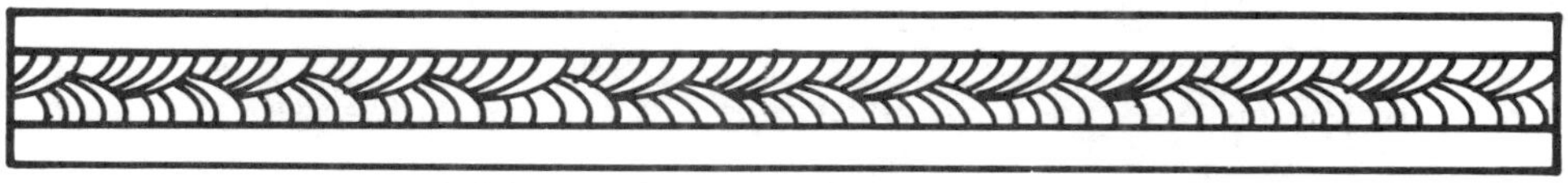

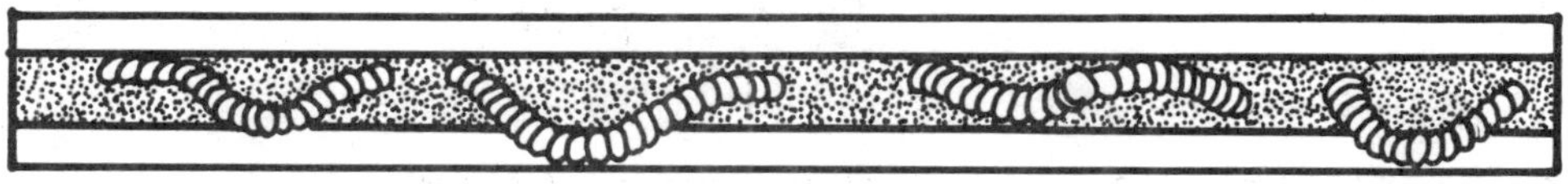

Texture 1 - Hammered

The hammered texture, on a soldered seam, gives the appearance of thousands of tiny craters. The texture, when patined, gives a dull background appearance. If patined and polished, the high ridges around the craters shine brightly against the lows of the craters. This texture is lovely when used as the only texture on a piece. It is an excellent background texture for many of the raised smooth textures given in further instructions. It offers a dull background for their brightly polished features.

Applications

1. An excellent background texture for raised polished textures.
2. A good masculine texture, not too flowery.
3. Used for subtle emphasis of an area.
4. Resembles sand, dirt or pebbles. Good texture for use around ground pieces.
5. Because it remains somewhat dark when polished, it is also a good texture to use on objects that appear in the background.
6. A good overall texture for jewelry. Accents should be added over it.
7. Very effective on vase caps and lamp bases.

Helpful Hints

1. Always be generous with the flux.
2. Tap quickly, do not allow iron to sink too deeply into seam.
3. Move around on the seam. Overworking an area causes meltdowns.
4. If hammering causes sharp peaks, re-flux and try again. If that does not work, raise the temperature of your iron by adjusting the temperature of the rheostat about 5%.
5. If your texture keeps melting down or away, you should lower the temperature setting about 5%.
6. Keep your soldering tip clean by wiping it on a wet sponge.
7. If hammering a narrow outside edge, the temperature must be as low as possible. Be sure to have a good solder buildup on the edge. You may also find that using the 1/8" tip on edges works best.

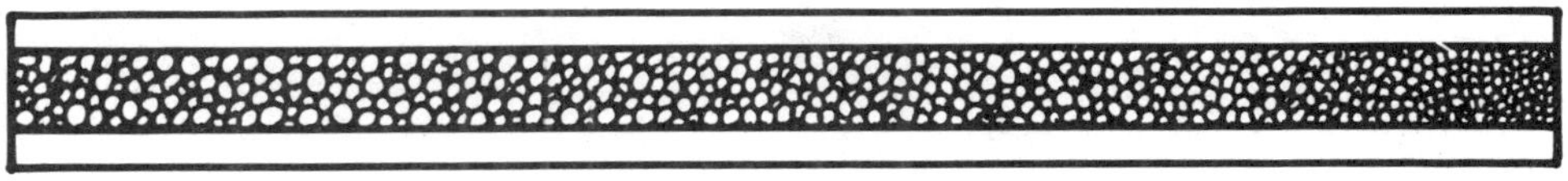

BASE BEAD . . . . .BASIC
TIP SIZE . . . . 1/8″
SOLDER. 60/40
TEMPERATURE SETTING 85%

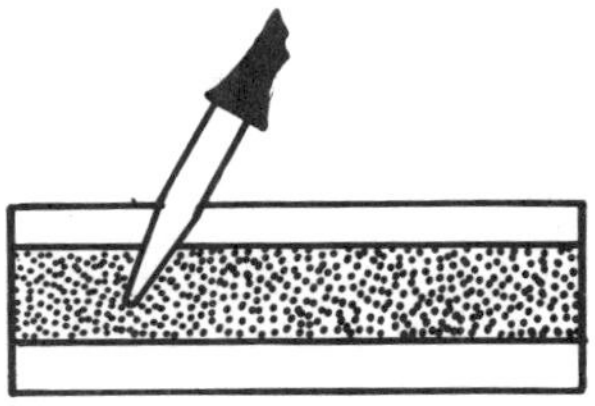

Instructions

1. Flux seam generously. Begin to gently tap the solder with the corner of the soldering iron. Tapping should be just hard enough to break the surface, but must not melt down the surrounding area. Tap quickly and lightly. Tap in a rythmic motion.

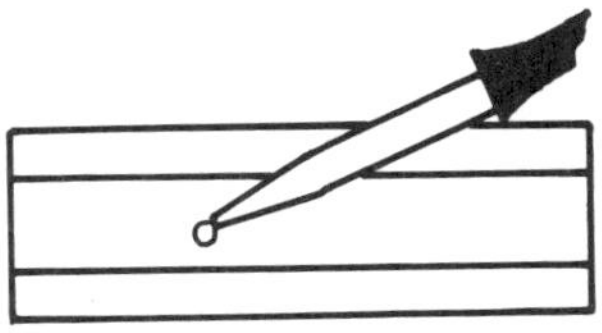

2. Tap seam so that indentations are sparsely placed along the entire seam. Do not concentrate tapping in one area as this will cause meltdown of the texture.

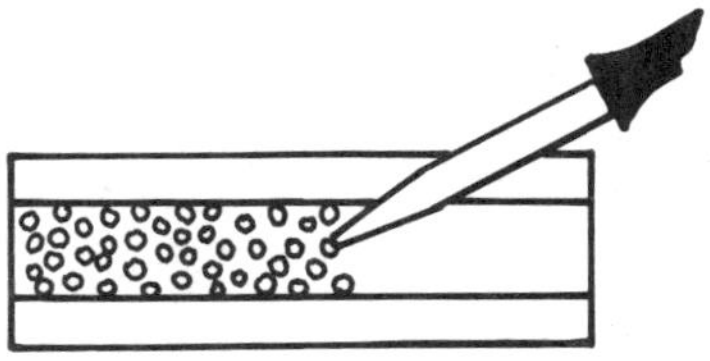

3. Go back over a previously tapped area to add additional texture. Repeat this process until the seam is heavily and evenly textured.

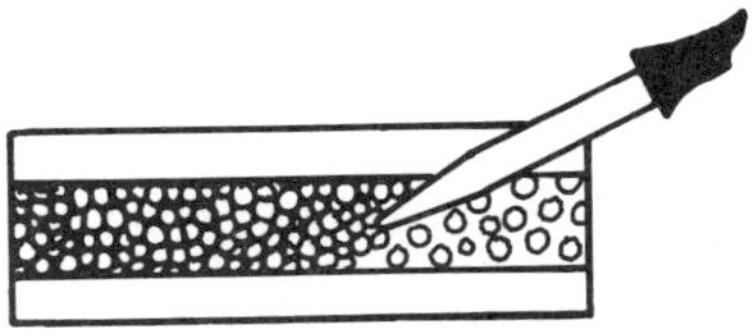

Texture 2 - Cascade

The Cascade, like the hammered, texture is worked into an existing solder bead. It looks somewhat like scuff marks in leather. The indentations are elongated, rather than round. The texture may be executed in a random direction or with the scuffs or scratches running in the same direction. When patined and polished it takes on a wispy weathered look. It is used to resemble feathers. It makes an excellent background texture.

Applications

1. An excellent texture to use as a background behind raised and polished textures.

2. A very natural texture. Good for use around furry or feathered animals. Use to surround plant pieces.

3. Resembles tree bark if done deeply and in a random pattern.

Helpful Hints

1. Always be generous with the flux.

2. Tap quickly. Do not allow the iron to sink too deeply into the basic bead.

3. Move around on the seam. Overworking an area can cause a texture meltdown.

4. If sharp peaks are produced, reflux the area and try again. If peaks still appear raise the temperature of your iron about 5%

5. If your texture keeps melting down or away lower the temperature of your rheostat about 5%.

6. Keep your soldering iron tip clean.

7. If you wish to add a cascade texture to the outside edge of a piece you must work very quickly and lower the temperature of your rheostat as much as possible. Using the 1/8" tip is also a good idea. Be sure to work on an edge that is well rounded with solder.

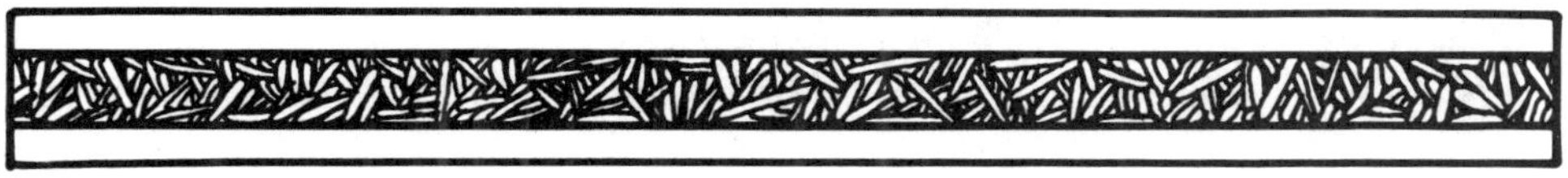

BASE BEAD . . . . .BASIC
TIP SIZE . . . . .1/8"
SOLDER. 60/40
TEMPERATURE SETTING 85%

Instructions

1. Flux the seam to be soldered generously. This texture is done in the same manner as hammering. It must be done quickly. Instead of tapping directly down and up, you must move the iron slightly as you lift the iron up. This gives you an elongated impression rather than the round impression of hammering. It can be moved in the same or in a random direction depending on the effect that you wish to achieve. The motion that you should be using is a scratching motion.

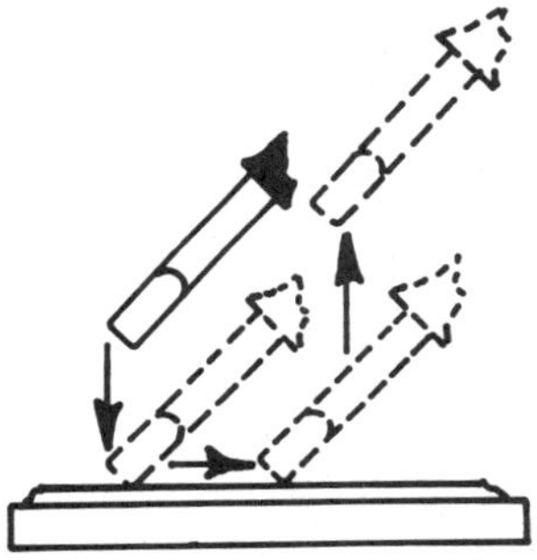

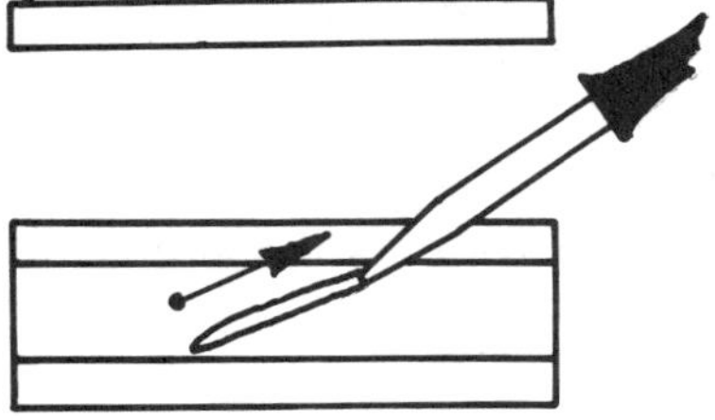

2. As in the hammering technique, you should work only a little at a time in any one spot. Texture lightly along the entire seam.

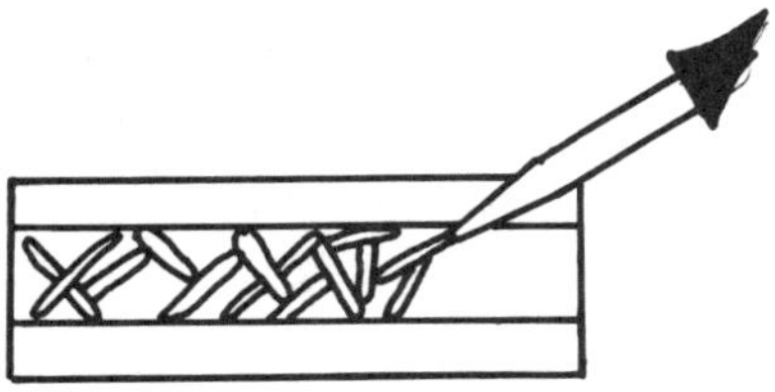

3. Go back over the seam repeatedly until the desired density of texture is achieved.

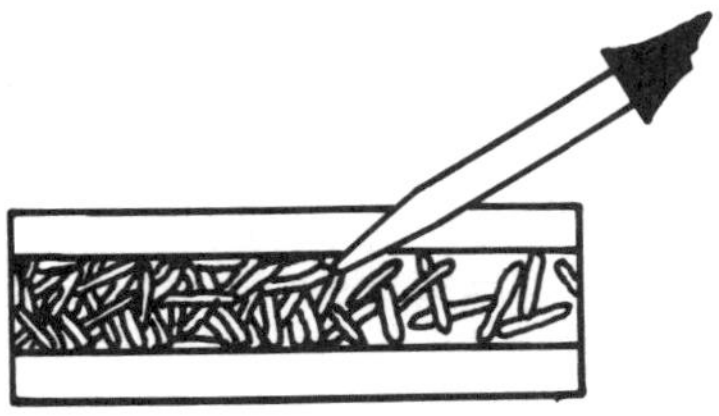

Texture 3 - Bamboo

Bamboo is a very basic and quick texture. It resembles the high-low texture of bamboo. Because of its ease of application it is a good overall texture for structures. It is a good texture to use for learning and perfecting consistency in solder application.

Applications

1. Because of the speed of application of this texture it is an excellent overall texture for large structures.
2. A good texture for borders of window panels.
3. Good for wood and large foliage pieces.
4. Can be used to resemble rope.

Helpful Hints

1. Always use a generous amount of flux.
2. Size can be regulated by the size of the tip; small tips give a smaller texture; larger tips give a larger texture.
3. Always approach the seam from the same perpendicular (90 degree) angle.
4. Do not hold the iron too flat with respect to the work surface as this will allow the glob to flatten out too much.
5. Holding the iron down to the surface too long will cause the glob to flatten too much.
6. Low temperature settings will cause the solder glob to remain higher and more exaggerated. Higher temperatures will cause the glob to flatten and lose definition.

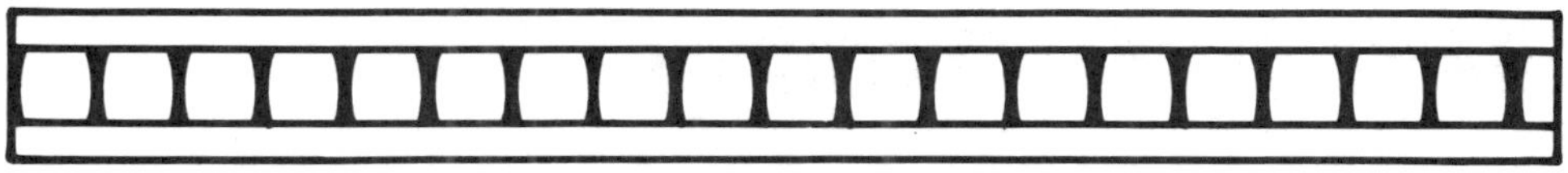

BASE BEAD . . . . .TIN ONLY
TIP SIZE . . . . .3/16"
SOLDER. 60/40
TEMPERATURE SETTING 90%

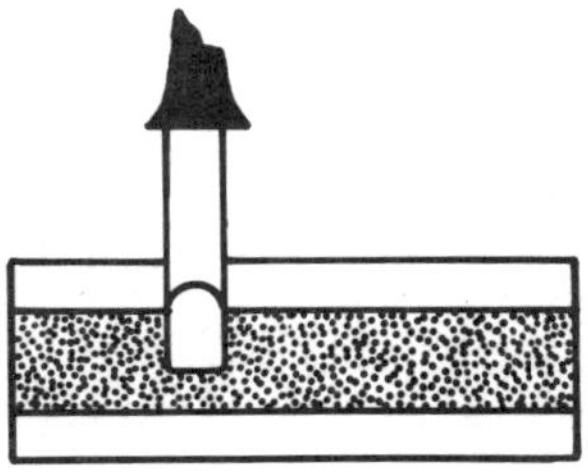

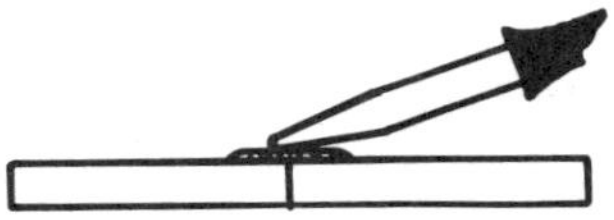

Instructions

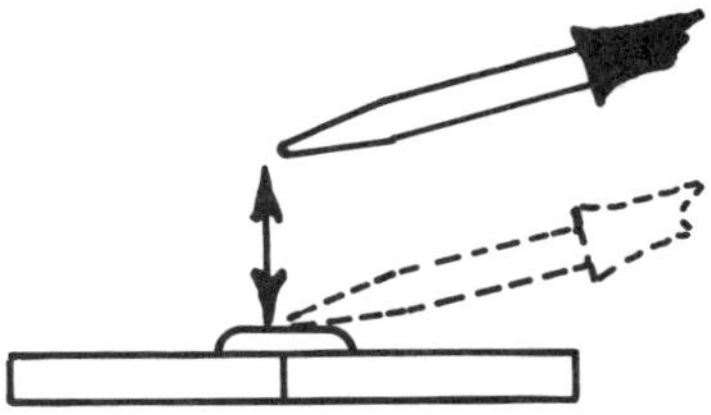

1. Flux thoroughly. Take 1/8" of solder and apply it as a glob to the beginning of the seam to be textured. The iron should appraoch at 90 degrees to the seam. The solder should be applied to the center of the seam. The iron should be held on the seam just long enough to apply the solder. The solder should spread no more than 1/4".

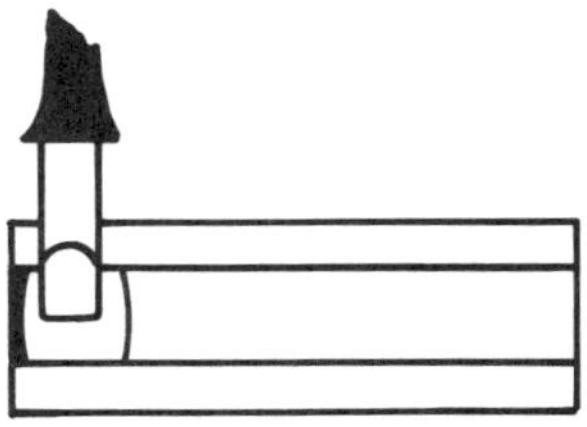

2. Take another 1/8" glob of solder and apply it to the seam about 1/8" from the first. The solder should be allowed to flow back to the first glob BUT NOT INTO IT.

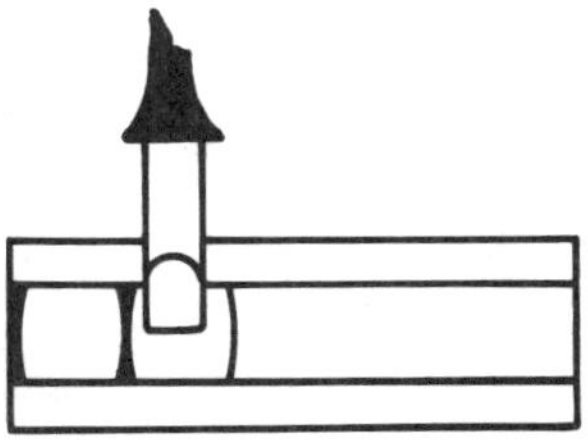

3. Continue setting globs of solder until the entire line has been layed. REMEMBER—DO NOT ALLOW GLOBS TO FLOW INTO EACH OTHER. If a glob does melt into another you may simply melt it away cleanly and continue.

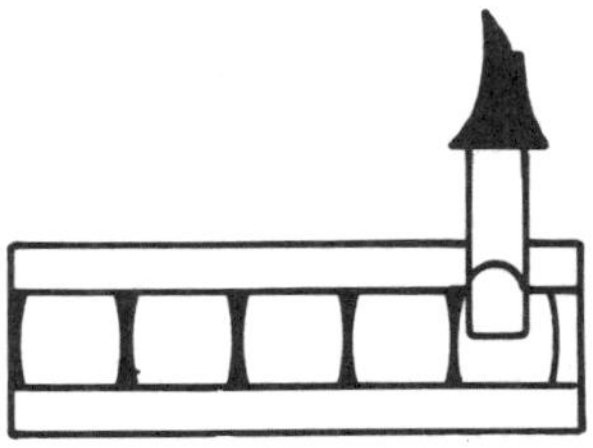

Texture 4 - Scallops

Scallops are low, rounded, raised areas added to a smooth or textured background. They can be done large or small, in runs of consistent size or in alternating sizes. They can be applied to one or both edges of a solder bead. They are highly decorative and used frequently in decorating jewelry boxes. They require good solder control.

Applications

1. Highly decorative, basically used to accent focal points on simple structures.
2. Excellent for jewelry boxes and small structures.
3. Most effective when applied over a textured background. This yields a beautiful contrast of bright and dull when patined and polished.
4. An excellent texture for jewelry.
5. Frequently used on vase caps and lamp bases.
6. Used to surround jewels or stones.
7. Generaly not used in natural scenes. Best used on whimsical subject matter only.

Helpful Hints

1. For control, it helps if you rest the bottom of your palm on the work board.
2. If a scallop is too small, add a little solder.
3. It is better to have a scallop a little small and simply add a little solder than to try to remove some. You will have to re-surface the background bead if you remove a scallop.
4. By having a background that is hammered or cascaded, you can easily re-surface a small area around a scallop that has been removed, thus making repair relatively easy.
5. Holding the iron perpendicular to the edge of the seam will create a scallop that is very round. If you apply a scallop with the corner of the tip, it will be more pointed in appearance.

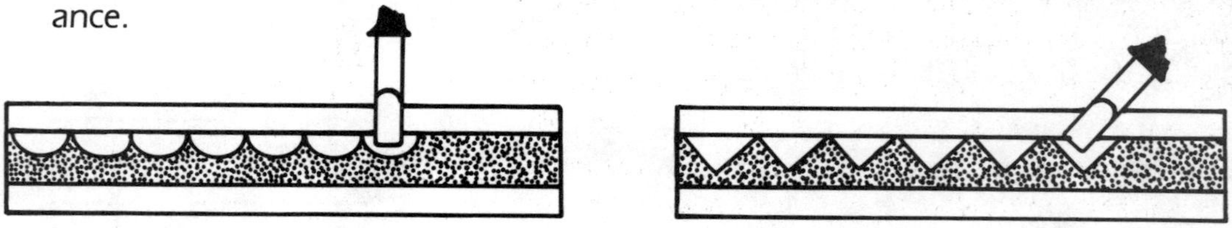

6. The size of the tip determines the size of the finished scallop. Small tips make small scallops; Large tips make large scallops.
7. Scallops can be placed on one or both edges of a seam.
8. If you desire the scallop to extend well into the seam you should apply the solder slightly into the base bead. Scallops that you want to stay close to the edge of the base bead should be applied to the edge of the basic bead itself.
9. As with most other textures, you should work quickly to avoid texture meltdowns.

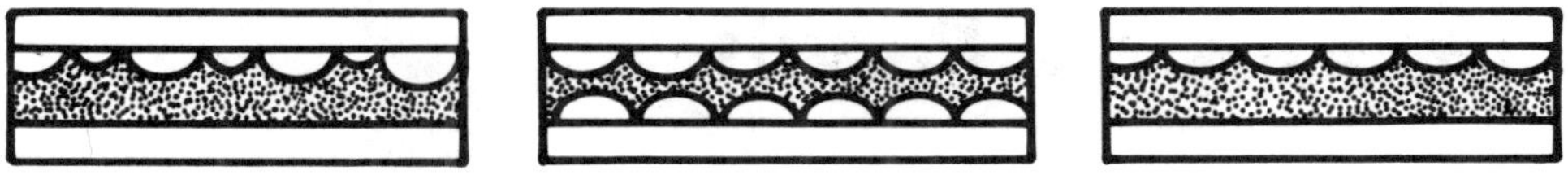

BASE BEAD. . . . . .BASIC (either smooth or textured)
TIP SIZE . . . . .1/8"
SOLDER. 63/37
TEMPERATURE SETTING 80%

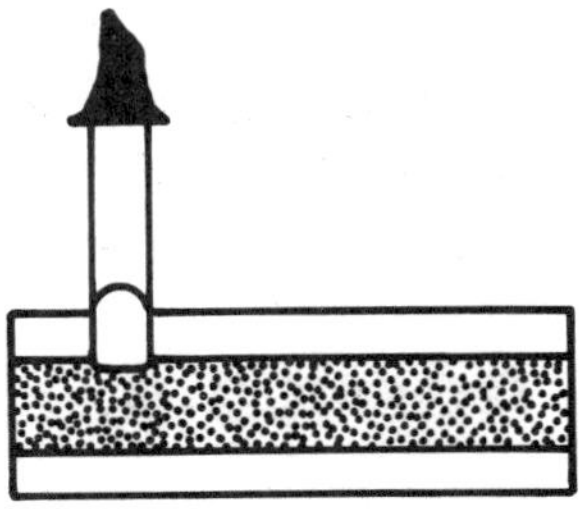

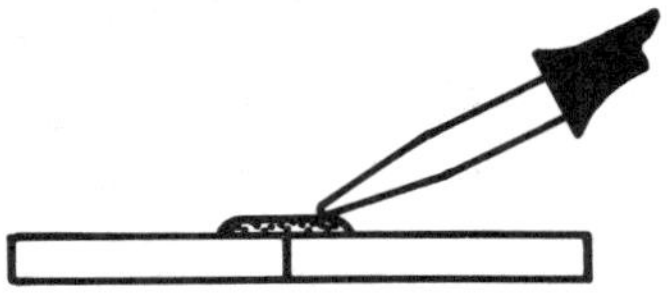

Instructions

1. Generously flux the bead to be scalloped. Take a tiny amount of solder with the end of your soldering tip. Apply it just slightly inward of the edge of the solder bead to be textured. The tiny solder glob should be just set into the basic bead. Allow the solder to spread slightly, forming a semi-circle shape on the surface of the basic bead. Do not allow the solder around the scallop to melt down. Work with speed and accuracy.

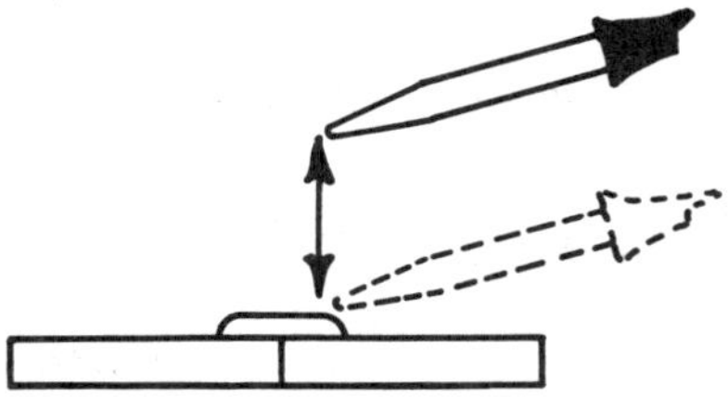

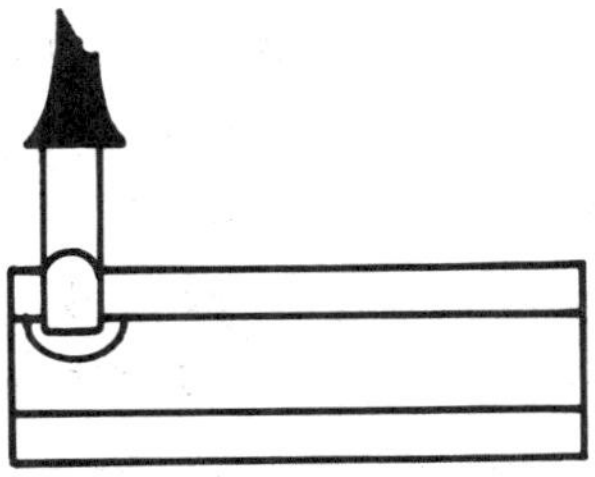

2. Place the second scallop near the first. It should spread to a point directly next to the first, but not touching. Be sure to use the same amount of solder and position it in the same way. If the second scallop is too large use less solder. Add solder to scallops that are too small. It is easier to add a little solder than to have to remove a scallop that is too large.

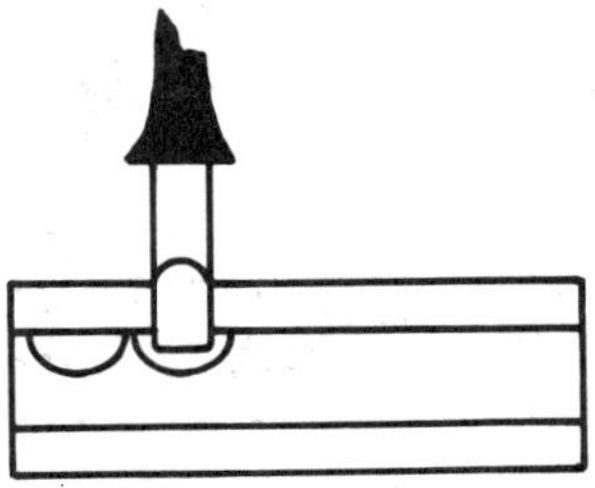

3. All other scallops should be done in the same manner along the seam being textured. If you are going to use scallops of the same size along a seam they must be exactly the same size. If you are going to do a pattern of alternating sizes they must alternate consistently.

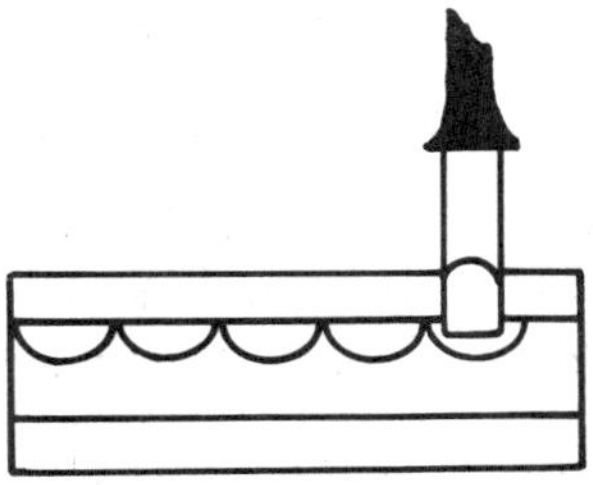

Texture 5 - Pearls

The Pearl texture is achieved by the addition of small drops of solder onto a basic bead or another texture, such as the centers of scallops. They often resemble "BBs" embedded slightly in the solder bead.

With pearls you can add great emphasis to an area. They are highly decorative.

Applications

1. A highly decorative texture.
2. Used primarily to decorate wire loops, knobs, and legs.
3. Jewelry is accented well with pearls.
4. Can be used over a hammered background to resemble pebbles in the sand.
5. When clustered they resemble gravel.
6. When used on lamps or other structures they accent beautifully.

Helpful Hints

1. If pearls flatten too much, you are probably holding the iron too long and too close to the basic bead.
2. By lowering the temperature you can also minimize meltdown.
3. If pearls fail to stick to the basic bead you are not allowing it to initially melt into the basic bead. Try barely tapping the basic bead while dropping off the solder.
4. When adding pearls to a bead or pre-existing texture the surface must be clean and freshly fluxed.
5. Pearl sizes may be varied by changing tip sizes or by slowly adding solder a little at a time. The latter method is the safest way to create larger pearls as they are harder to melt down when built up gradually.
6. CLEANING, PATINING, AND POLISHING OF PEARLS CAN BE DIFFICULT. SINGLE PEARLS OR LINES OF PEARLS POSE LITTLE PROBLEM BUT CLUSTERS CREATE LARGE VOIDS IN WHICH CHEMICALS CAN LODGE. FOR THIS REASON WE ADVOCATE USING PEARLS SPARINGLY.

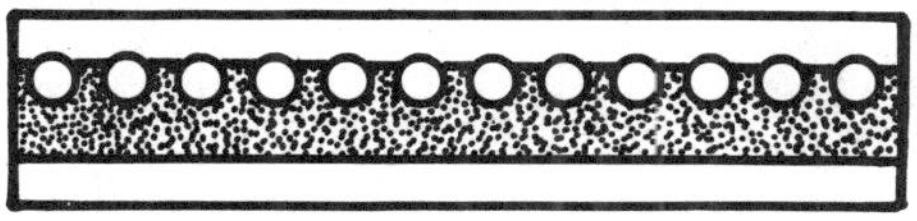

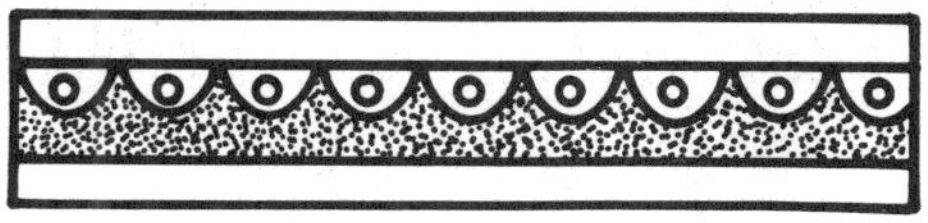

BASE BEAD . . . . .BASIC (SMOOTH OR TEXTURED) OR ADD TO ANOTHER TEXTURE.
TIP SIZE. . . . . .1/8" (LARGER FOR LARGER PEARLS)
SOLDER. 63/37
TEMPERATURE SETTING 80%

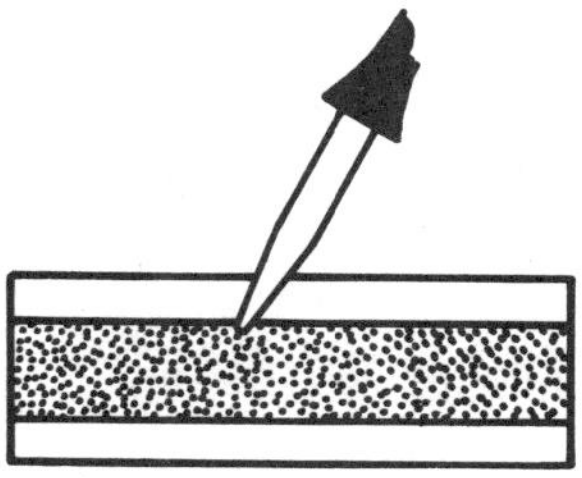

Instructions

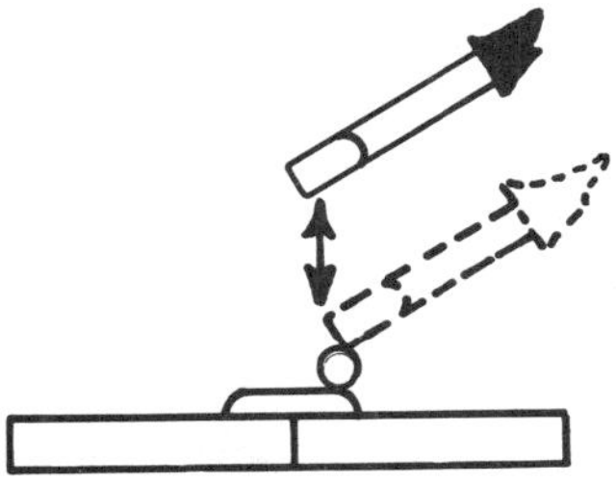

1. Generously flux area to be textured. Take a small amount of solder with the corner of your tip. Touch the basic bead with the solder until it attaches itself to the bead. The iron really shouldn't make prolonged contact with the basic bead. You should lift the iron immediatly to prevent the pearls from melting down into the basic bead.

2. All other pearls are added where you desire them in the same manner. Larger pearls may be created by adding a little more solder to a smaller pearl. If you try to make a large pearl immediately it may melt down before it solidifies.

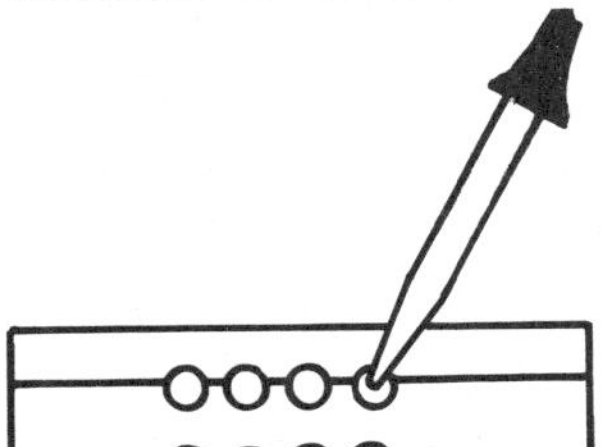

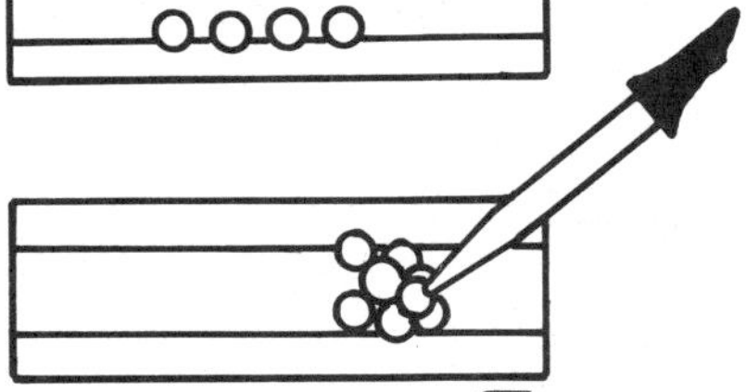

3. Pearls may be clustered on top of one another by refluxing the area and quickly adding small pearls close to or on top of other pearls which have already cooled. Work quickly as they can melt together.

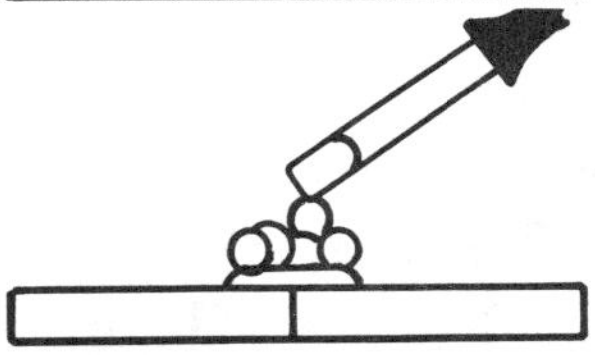

Texture 6 - Herringbone

The Herringbone texture is comprised of pointed scallops placed on alternating opposite edges of a basic bead. This texture requires great solder control to create an effective finished texture. It is very elegant in its simplicity when executed properly. It resembles braided rope when done right.

Applications

1. Makes a good border texture.
2. Good to use on the seams of jewelry boxes.
3. Resembles rope, braid, and twisted vines.
4. A good masculine texture, not too flowery.

Helpful Hints

1. If "scallops" round out, you should be sure that you are holding the iron at a 45 degree angle to the edge of the seam.
2. If the "scallops" do not flow 3/4 of the way across the seam use a little more solder and/or check that you are placing the solder 1/4 of the way into the seam. Make sure that you hold the iron down long enough to allow the solder to flow.
3. If "scallops" extend all the way across the seam, use a little less solder and/or be sure that your iron is not too far into the seam.
4. Follow the instructions for scallops to regulate the size, height and flow of the herringbone scallops. Remember that the angle at which you hold the iron regulates whether you achieve a pointed scallop.
5. If the "scallops" are larger on one edge of the seam than the other, you must adjust your procedure so as to ensure consistency on both edges.
6. If the "scallops" applied on the second edge of the seam flow into the "scallops" on the first edge, you should lower the temperature and/or use slightly less solder. Be sure that you are not holding the iron down too long, as this too will cause a meltdown.

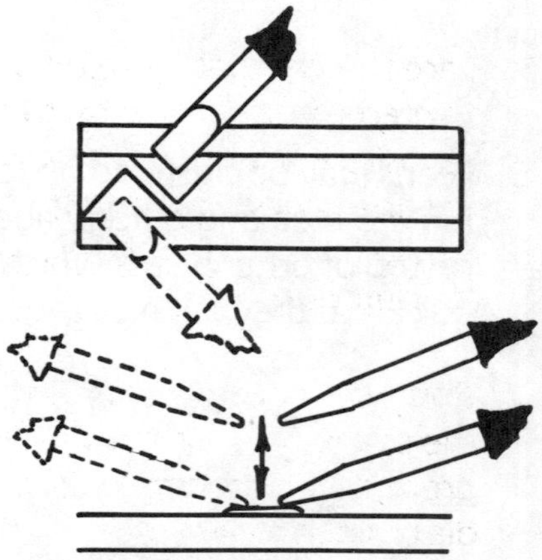

Instructions

1. Flux seam to be textured. Take about 1/16" of solder with your iron. Place the first glob of solder onto the seam with the iron held at a 45 degree angle to the seam. The tip should be placed about 1/4 of the seam width into the seam. The solder should flow, like when doing a scallop, along the seam slightly. It should move inward from the

BASE BEAD . . . . .FLAT OR LOW BASIC
TIP SIZE . . . . .1/8"
SOLDER. 60/40
TEMPERATURE SETTING 85%

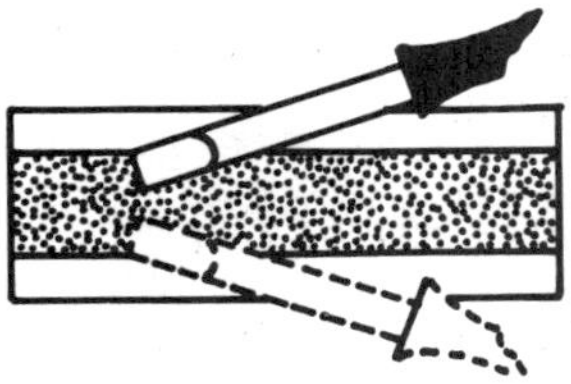

edge 3/4 of the way across the seam. However, it should not move entirely across the seam.

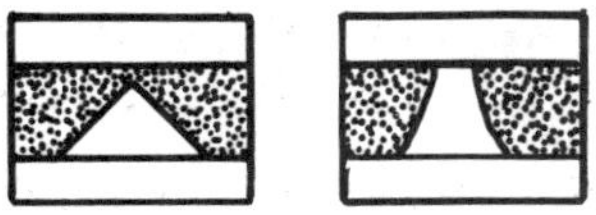

2. The second glob is applied next to, but not touching, the first. It should flow to the same size and shape as the first. Idealy the "scallops" that you are creating should be the same size as the voids created on the opposite edge of the seam.

3. Continue adding these "pointed" scallops for the entire length of the seam. Be sure they are consistent.

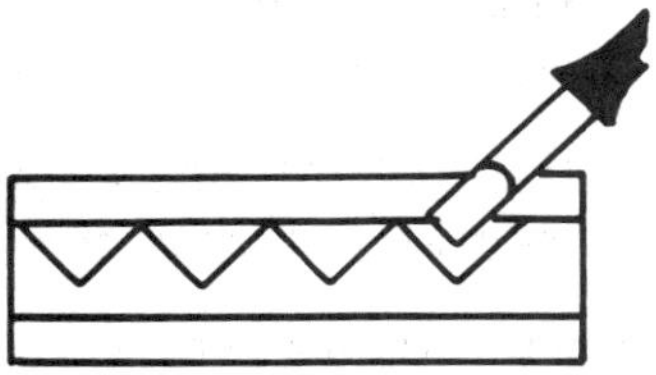

4. Turn the piece around so that you can approach the other edge of the seam from the same direction.

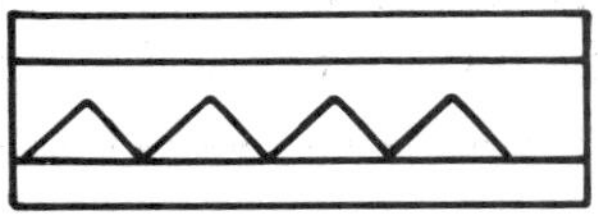

5. Place the first glob of solder in the same manner into the pointed space formed by the "pointed" scallops on the opposite edge of the seam. It should flow to the same size and shape as those on the opposite edge. They all should flow up to but not into the the "scallops" on the opposite edge.

6. Continue adding solder into the pointed spaces along the seam, until all spaces have been filled. The finished product should form a zig-zag pattern. It should resemble braided rope.

Texture 7 - Shells

This texture resembles a clustering of horn shaped seashells. It is very irregular and can be done as a flat, medium, or high texture. The flat can be used as a background texture. The medium and high textures are used as decorative accents.

This texture is difficult and requires good solder flow and iron control. The size, shape, and depth of the texture is affected by the temperature, amount of solder, and your control of the soldering iron.

Since it is an irregular texture a seam can consist of unevenly shaped, sized and directional shells. Shells can be layered on top of each other for even more definition. Remember that the more pronounced the textural differences the greater difficulty you may have in cleaning, patining and polishing.

You will have to do a lot of experimentation with this technique in order to achieve the desired effect.

63/37 SOLDER IS A MUST, AS THE SUCCESS OF THIS TEXTURE DEPENDS ON THE QUICK SOLIDIFICATION OF THE SOLDER.

Applications

1. Used to border pieces in seascapes.
2. Resembles heavy bark when used around trees.
3. An excellent texture to use on small and simple structures.
4. A must for jewelry.
5. As a flat background-type texture it is beautiful on vase caps and lamp bases.
6. The flat texture makes a covered vase, goblet or candlestick appear antique.

Helpful Hints

1. You may want to work various areas along the seam to prevent meltdowns. Since the pattern is random you do not have to worry about spacing.
2. The cooler the iron the less chance of meltdowns. This will also enable the solder to solidify quickly, ensuring a well- defined shell. When using a cooler iron be sure that you do not form sharp peaks at the ends of the shells.
3. Flux frequently. This helps in maintaining the definition of the shells.
4. You will probably have to experiment with the temperature settings, tip size, and angle of the iron before you perfect the shells.

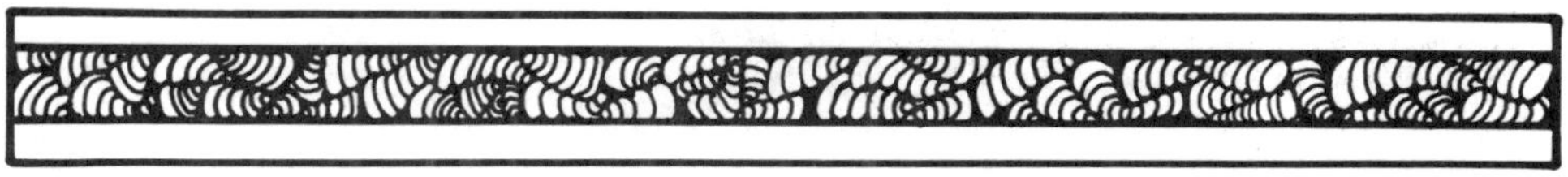

BASE BEAD . . . . FLAT
TIP SIZE . . . . . . 1/8" (UNLESS WORKING ON A LARGE SURFACE)
SOLDER 63/37
TEMPERATURE SETTING 75%

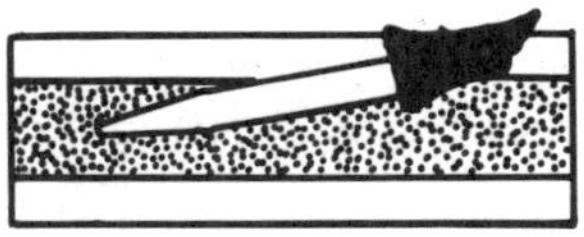

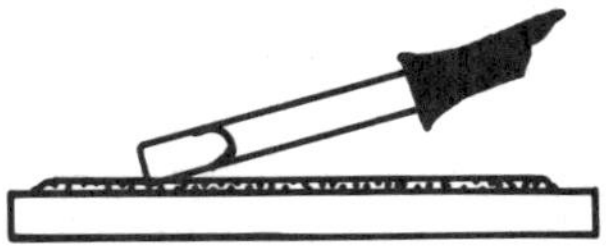

Instructions

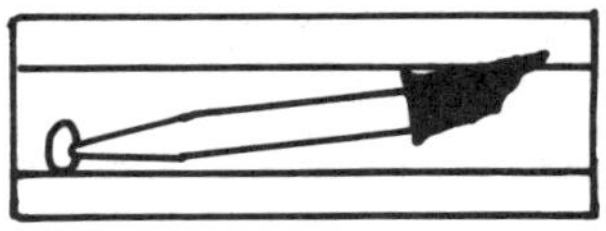

1. Flux the seam well. Hold the iron as shown in the first illustration for small shells. With your iron, add a small amount of solder onto the seam and draw the iron away from the initial touchdown point. As you draw it away, repeatedly and quickly tap it against the seam. This will cause the solder to solidify in a rippled manner.
   You should also be drawing the tip slightly upward away from the surface as you tap. This causes the tail of the shell to become narrower.
   Continue drawing the soldering iron up and away, while still tapping, until you have run out of solder and have formed a ridged, conical-shaped texture. The number of taps depends on how much solder you have to dispense. If you are using the corner of an 1/8" tip the shell should be well defined.
   A finished small shell should be no longer than 3/8", and 1/8" at its widest point, tapering to nothing at the end. In a shell of that size you probably will have tapped 8 to 10 times.

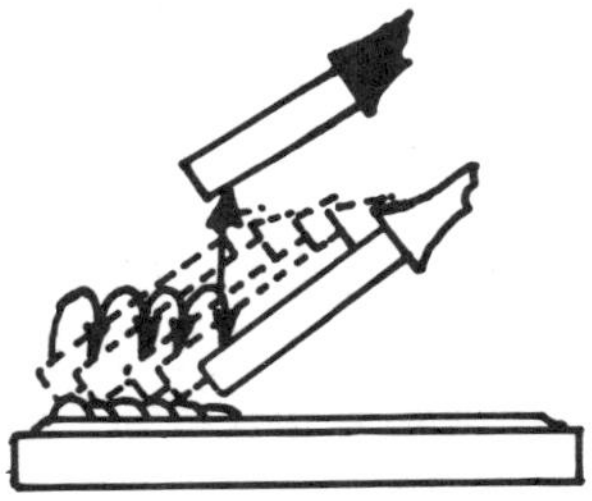

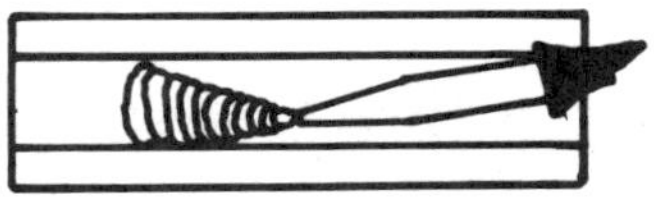

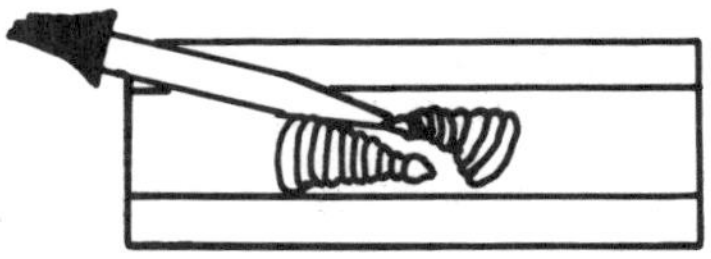

2. The second shell should be formed in the same manner, near the first shell. Unless you are using the shell as an accent along the edge of a seam, the second shell should be facing in a different direction and have a slightly different size and shape. This is easy to achieve because it is very hard to be consistent with shells.

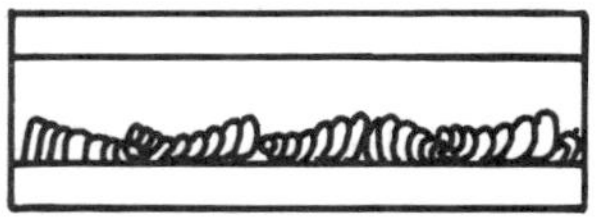

3. Continue adding randomly placed shells along the length of the seam. Additional shells can be added onto the first layer for more depth and definition. You must work quickly to prevent meltdown of the first layer.

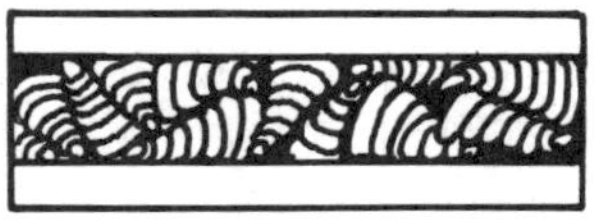

Texture 8 - Wheat

The Wheat texture is a combination of Herringbone and Shells. It is very controlled and should be attempted only after you have mastered both. It is accomplished by laying flat shells, like the scallops in herringbone, on alternating and opposite edges of a seam. It requires great solder control and a quick and rhythmic touch.

Applications

1. A subtle overall seam texture.
2. Resembles rope.
3. Use on borders.
4. A good texture for masculine projects.

Helpful Hints

1. Consistency and control are of utmost importance.
2. Be generous with the flux.
3. Cool temperature setting is essential. Meltdown is common if your iron is too hot.
4. Too much solder causes the texture to become too bulky and lose its subtle beauty.
5. You must work quickly and rhythmically.
6. Remember to tap the same number of times during each solder application.
7. Be sure that the angle of the soldering iron is the same for each solder application.
8. BE PATIENT—THIS IS A DIFFICULT TEXTURE.
9. THIS TEXTURE CAN ONLY BE USED WITHIN THE CONFINES OF A SEAM. IT CANNOT BE ADAPTED OR MODIFIED FOR USE ON LARGE AREAS. IT ALSO IS HARD TO ACHIEVE ON VERY NARROW SEAMS.

Instructions

WE USUALLY WORK THIS TEXTURE WITH THE SEAM RUNNING TOWARDS US. WE START AT THE FARTHEST POINT AND WORK TOWARDS US. THIS ENABLES YOU TO ACHIEVE THE TEXTURE WITHOUT REPOSITIONING THE PIECE.

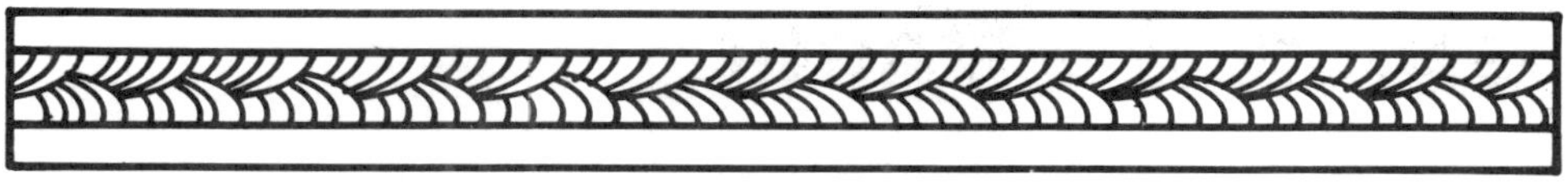

BASE BEAD . . . . .FLAT
TIP SIZE . . . . .3/16″ or 1/8″
SOLDER. 63/37
TEMPERATURE SETTING 65%

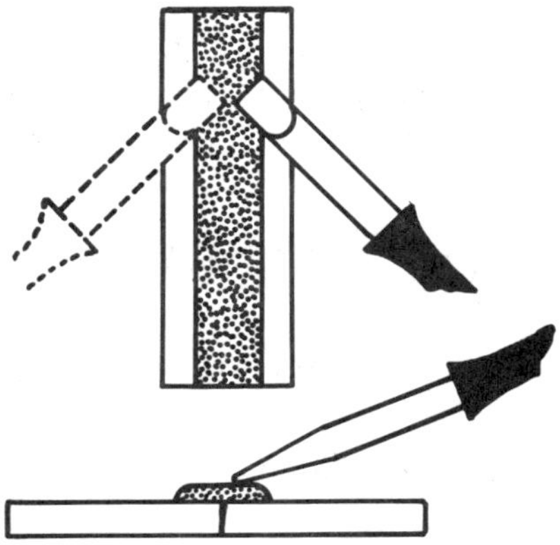

1. Flux well. Place a small amount of solder on the seam, as you did with herringbone, but you should apply it halfway into the seam. Instead of removing your iron immediately, draw it down towards you and outward towards the edge of the seam. This is done using three additional taps. This should have formed a flat, shell-shaped scallop along the edge of the seam.

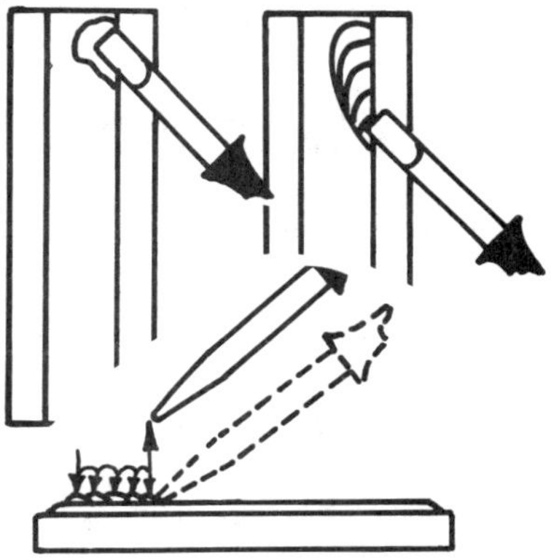

2. The second application of solder is added to the opposite edge of the seam, about halfway down the initial textured glob. Be sure the iron is again at a 45 degree angle to the seam and halfway into the seam. Again draw the iron down and out towards the seam edge, tapping three additional times.

3. Continue this procedure, switching from side to side each time, until the entire seam has been textured. The first four or five globs do not appear to form much of a texture. As you proceed down the seam, the texture becomes more apparent.

BE PATIENT — THIS TEXTURE TAKES THE MASTERY OF TWO TEXTURES SO IT IS ACTUALLY TWICE AS HARD TO LEARN AS THE OTHERS.

Texture 9 - Wrap

The Wrap technique is the application of a narrow, rippled, raised texture diagonally across a raised basic bead (either smooth or textured). These "Wraps" are spaced approximately 1/4" apart and should be placed at a consistent angle across the base bead. Wraps resemble rope. If randomly placed they resemble vinework.

Applications

1. If applied randomly, the wrap resembles vines.
2. Consistently spaced wraps resemble rope.
3. It can be used on seams within jewelry.
4. An interesting effect can be achieved when used on structural projects i.e., jewelry boxes, terrariums, many lamps, etc.

Helpful Hints

1. If your wrap melts into the base bead lower the temperature. Working the solder too slowly also can cause meltdowns.
2. If the wrap spreads out too much initially, try using a little less solder or lower temperature.
3. It is easier to add on than to erase.
4. Work quickly and rhythmically.
5. To ensure a well-defined wrap, use only the corner of the soldering iron tip.

Instructions

1. Flux the base bead well. Take a small amount of solder on the corner of your tip. Begin at one edge of the base bead and lightly tap the corner of the iron, allowing the solder to set onto the bead. Gently draw the iron diagonally across the seam, dispensing the solder with a series of quick, gentle taps. The solder that you are dropping should rest on the base bead—it should not melt too deeply into the base. The wrap should be of consistent height and width across the entire seam. If you run out of solder before you reach the edge of the seam you may add a little more to your tip and begin just inside of

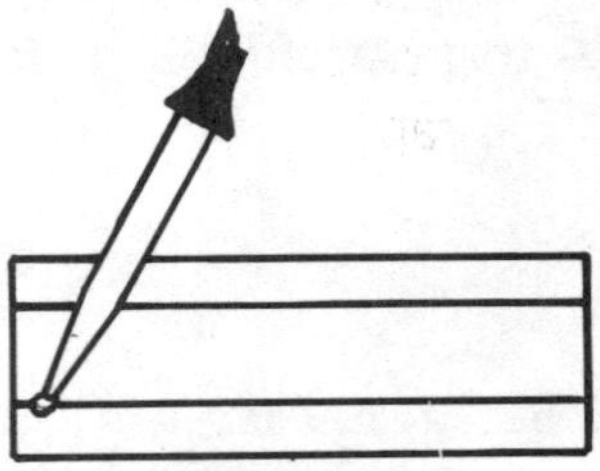

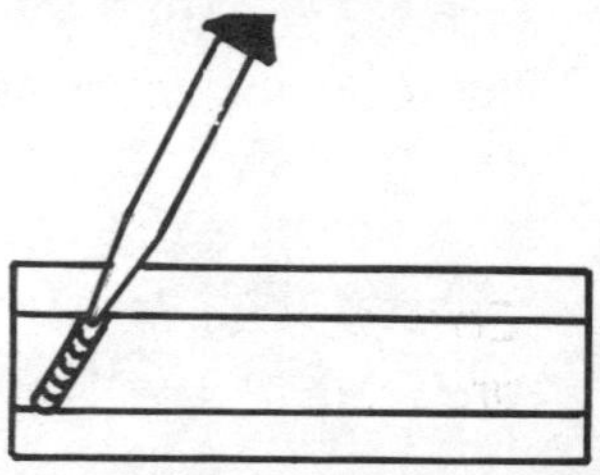

BASE BEAD. . . . . . . .BASIC (EITHER SMOOTH OR HAMMERED)
TIP. . . . . .1/8"
SOLDER. 63/37
TEMPERATURE SETTING 70%

where you ran out and continue to the edge. It is easy to add a little solder. It is hard to successfully repair a bad wrap. Using too much solder causes you to lose control of your wrap.

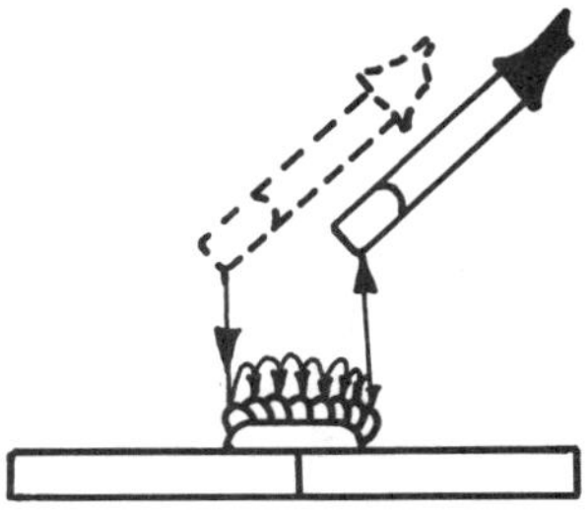

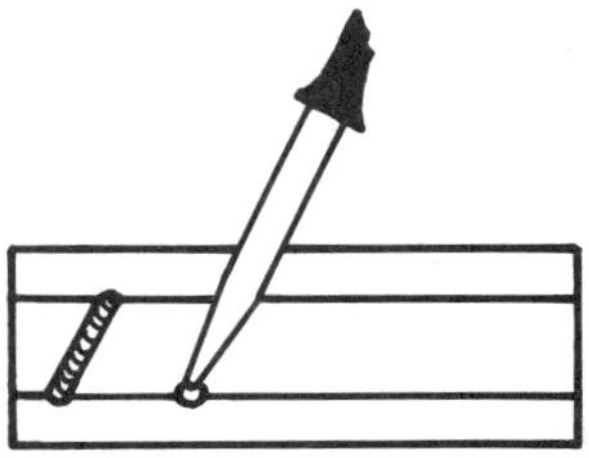

2. The second wrap is added about 1/4" down the base bead. It should be dispensed at the same angle as the first wrap.

3. Continue adding wraps until you have wrapped the entire seam.

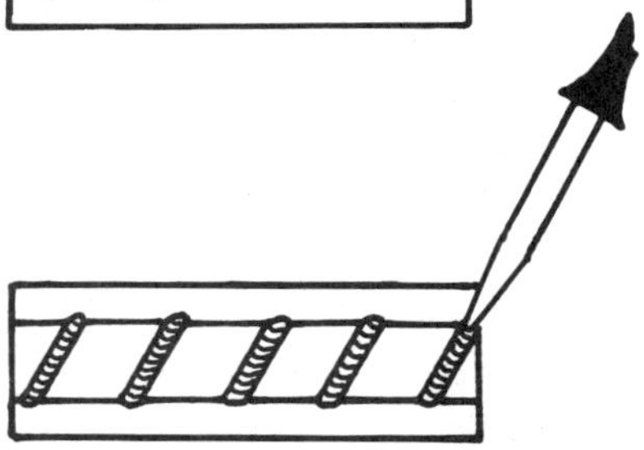

Texture 10 - Bridging

Bridging is not really a texture, but rather a method of building with solder. 63/37 solder should always be used because it solidifies quickly. It is a slow process since you must allow the solder to cool before adding additional solder. The best tip to use is the 1/8" tip, because you can more easily control the amount of solder you are applying.

Bridging is used to construct vinework, legs, drawer pulls, box lid lift knobs, and free-form sculpture.

Applications

1. Build from seam to seam to resemble vinework.
2. Build free-form legs, knobs and drawer pulls for boxes.
3. Use to wrap and hold in place stones or shells in jewelry making.
4. Use to hold things in place in free-form sculptures.

Helpful Hints

1. If the bridge does not seem to be growing and you keep adding solder, it is probably melting into itself. Let it cool down longer between applications. Add more flux or lower the temperature of the iron. Be sure that you are not trying to add too much solder.
2. If the solder you are adding does not stick to the bridge add more flux.
3. Be sure to make any directional changes gradually.
4. Remember that the bridge cannot get larger in diameter as it grows in length.
5. Construct your bridge from both ends.
6. Tilting your project can aid in directional changes.

Instructions

1. Flux the area to be built upon. Apply a very large glob of solder as the base for your bridge.

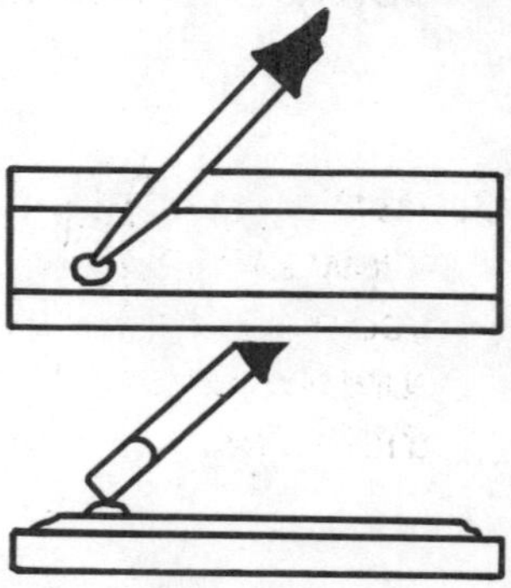

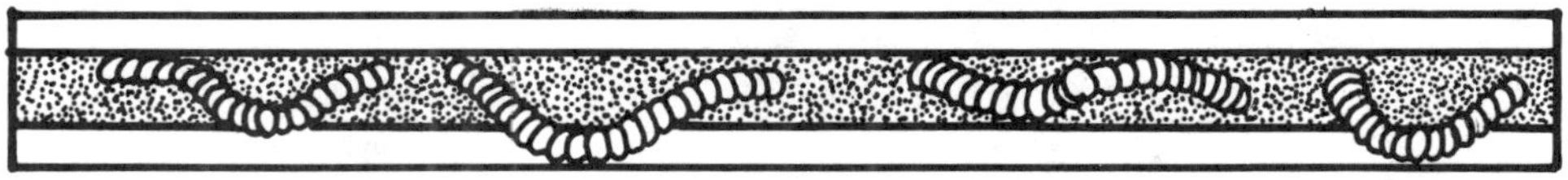

BASE BEAD . . . . .ANY
TIP . . . . .1/8"
SOLDER. 63/37
TEMPERATURE SETTING 80%

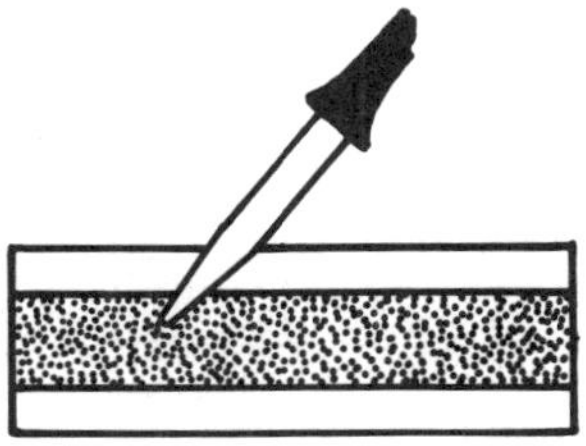

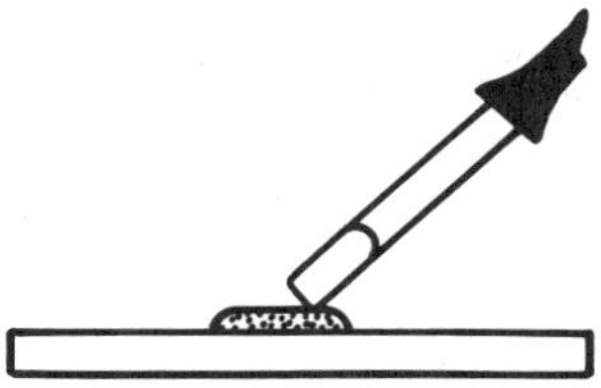

2. Flux again and add another glob of solder to the top of the initial glob. Drop it quickly. Do not allow it to melt down into the first. Another glob may now be added.

3. Allow the bridge to cool a few seconds. Two or three more globs may be added after refluxing.

4. Each addition of solder cannot be larger than the previous one. This will cause meltdowns.

5. You may start the second end of the bridge, building it as the first end cools.

6. If you need to have the bridge bend, change the angle slowly. Too abrupt a change can cause a collapse.

7. As the two ends of the bridge grow together you should allow them to cool longer between applications. When you place the last glob, linking the two ends together, be sure to reflux and be sure not to add too much solder as the bridge may collapse.

5 Variations and Combinations of Textures

Once you have mastered the basic textures, you should experiment with varying and combining them. This will enable you to create many new and exciting effects. You should be able to come up with the perfect texture for any application.

Variations are simply modifications of the basic textures and the techniques used to achieve them. They require changing tip sizes, temperature or the angle of the work surface itself. You will find that holding the soldering iron at a different angle, or approaching the solder bead from a different point will significantly change the texture. You may go back to the areas where you practiced and see some of the different appearances of the textures as you learned them. You may see that some scallops were too large. This was caused by too much heat, or too much solder, or changes in the size and angle of the soldering iron tip. You learned to regulate your scallop by changing one or more of the above factors. This method can be used to alter any of the basic textures to create new effects.

The tip size, as we have already briefly discussed, will change the size of the texture. For a larger scallop you use a larger tip; conversely, a smaller tip gives you a smaller scallop. That same scallop can be affected by the angle at which you hold your soldering iron. Holding an iron at a lower angle with respect to the work surface will give you a flatter and larger texture. A higher angle creates a higher and smaller texture.

The angle of the tip of the soldering iron with respect to its entry point on the basic solder bead also greatly affects the texture. Solder that is applied by the flat tip of an iron approaching the bead at 90 degrees will give a wide texture. If a texture is applied with the corner of the iron it will be smaller (see Fig. 5-A).

FIG. 5-A....Texture Width Adjustments

The further in on the basic bead you apply your solder the larger the texture will be. It will spread over a larger area. A scallop applied at the very edge of the basic bead will spread along the edge first and then inward on the bead. It will remain close to the edge allowing scallops to be added on both edges of the bead (see Fig. 5-B).

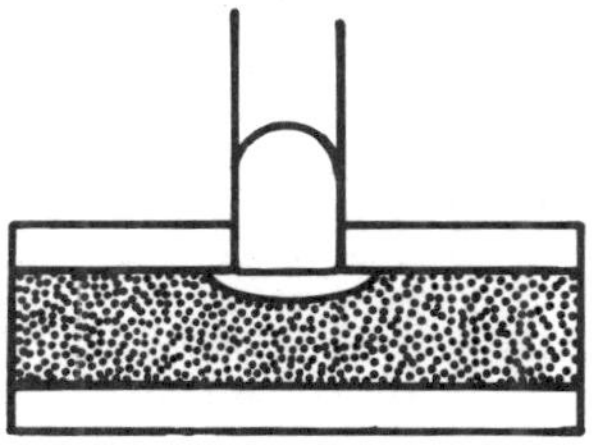

FIG. 5-B....Solder Applied To The Edge Of The Bead

If you add the solder slightly inward on the bead you will achieve a scallop that is large and deep into the basic bead. In this application you will generally only be able to scallop one edge of the bead (see Fig. 5-C).

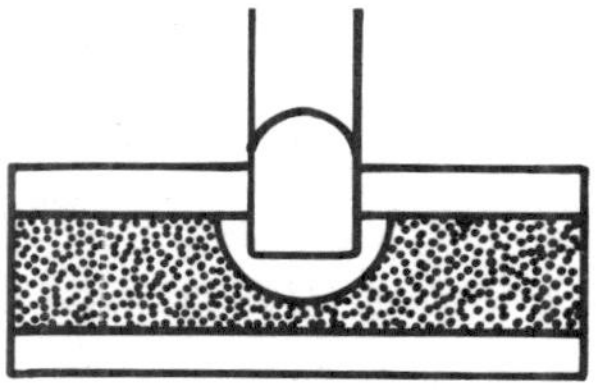

FIG. 5-C....Solder Applied Inward On The Bead

The most radical method of altering a texture is by slanting the object you are working on. This takes advantage of gravity in the alteration of the texture. It affects only a few textures but can be used quite effectively in some situations. BAMBOO and SCALLOPS are the two textures used in this method; but, with experimentation, you may find some others. The final appearance of a texture that is DRAPED or applied in this manner, is that the lower portion of the texture (with respect to the bottom of the slant) is higher (see Fig. 5-D). That is, each solder application of a texture has a high area and a low area.

FIG. 5-D....Side View Of Draped Bamboo

The angle at which you hold the object to be soldered affects the finished appearance. Flatter angles yield a less radical difference in the appearance of the texture. A piece that is held at 45 degrees or more will yield a very definite texture change. Flatter angles will produce a less noticeable change. See Fig. 5-E for some typical results of Draping Bamboo. Practice this technique at various angles to achieve the effect that you want.

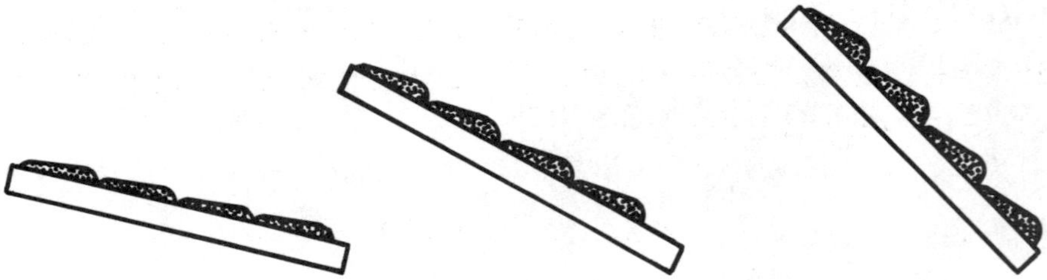

FIG. 5-E....Variations Of Draped Bamboo By Altering The Angle

The solder is applied in the same manner as you would in working on a flat surface. You start at the top of the bead and work downward. Each application of solder should be placed so that it does not touch the previous application, as this will cause them to run into each other and flow uncontrollably down your bead.

As you will probably find out, when experimenting with this technique, it is VERY important to be in control of the amount of solder that you use. Too much solder will cause a runaway bead. Too little will not give the desired draped effect.

It is VERY important that you keep the object you are working on at a consistent angle in order to maintain a uniform texture.

THIS DRAPED EFFECT IS VERY FUNCTIONAL WHEN WORKING ON STRUCTURES, AS YOU ELIMINATE SOME OF THE PROBLEMS OF LEVELING THE OBJECT THAT YOU ARE WORKING ON. YOU CAN NOW USE THE ANGLES OF THE OBJECT TO HELP CREATE THE TEXTURE.

The following instructions will help you achieve a Draped Bamboo texture.

1. Prepare the seam to be textured in the standard manner. Work with it level at this point.

2. Place the object you are working on at approximately a 45 degree angle to the work surface. Secure it against falling or changing angle.

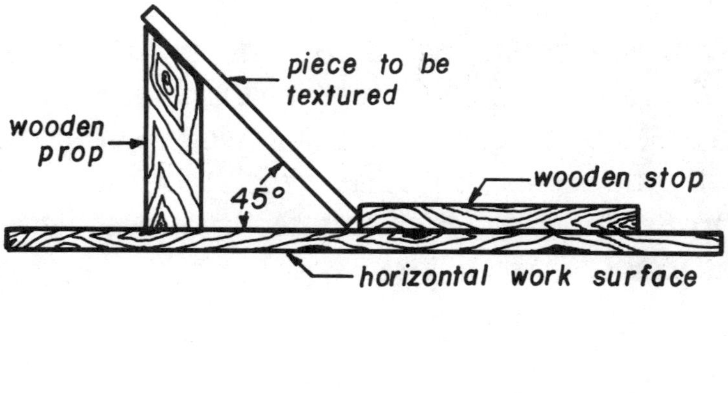

3. Place the first glob of solder at the top of the line to be soldered. Remove the iron. Note that the solder flows downward, forming a glob that is thicker or higher at the lower portion.

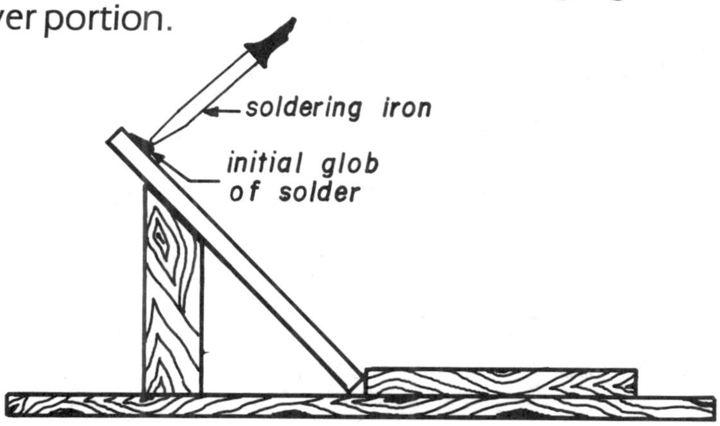

4. The second glob is added slightly below, but not touching, the first. Move it upward slightly towards the first until they almost touch. Remove the iron. That glob should drop at the same angle as the first. If the first is a different size than the second the amount of solder used was probably different. If the first glob melted into the second you allowed the two to touch. Next time don't let them get so close together.

5. Continue applying solder on down the bead. This will result in a Draped Bamboo bead. With practice you will achieve consistency.

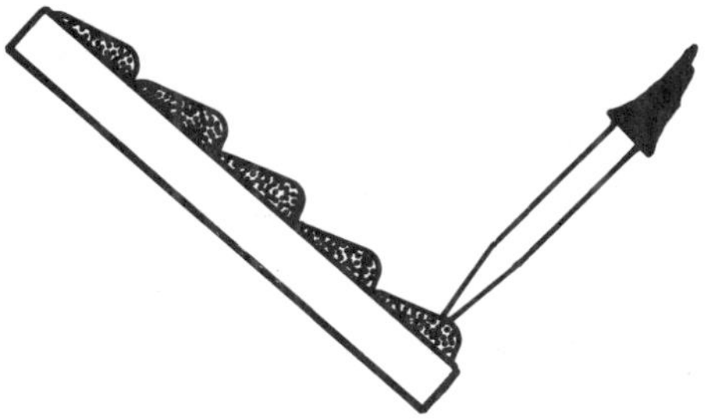

6. Try altering the angle of your object to see what different effects can be achieved.

SCALLOPS CAN BE DRAPED ONLY IF THEY ARE LARGE AND APPLIED OVER

A RELATIVELY LOW INITIAL BEAD. EXPERIMENT AND SEE WHAT YOU CAN ACHIEVE (See Fig. 5-F).

FIG. 5-F....Draped Scallops

Temperature, as we have already discussed, effects textures too. Basically, the lower the temperature the more dramatic and defined the texture. Care must be taken not to lower the temperature too much as this creates sharp peaks (see Fig. 5-G). When texturing with SHELLS finer detail can be achieved by lowering the tem-

FIG. 5-G....Effects Of Temperature Variance

perature. The texture will be higher and more defined. Flatter shells are achieved by raising the temperature. This allows the solder to smooth out more and thus give a flatter less-defined texture (see Fig. 5-H).

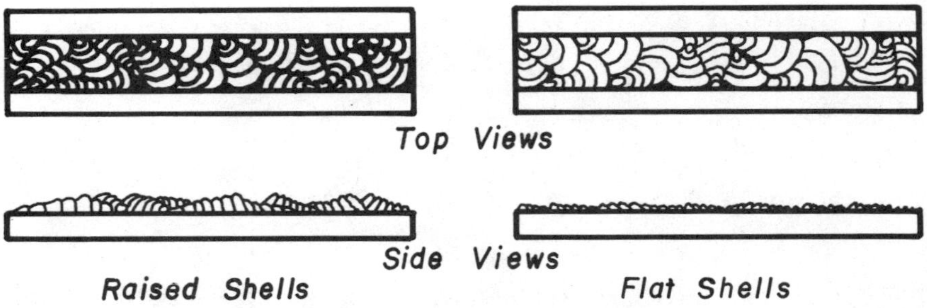

FIG. 5-H....Effects Of Temperature On Shells

REMEMBER THAT THE SIZE OF THE AREA TO BE SOLDERED WILL ALSO REQUIRE TEMPERATURE ADJUSTMENTS.

ALL VARIATIONS DISCUSSED ABOVE ARE GREATLY AFFECTED BY THE SIZE OF THE AREA BEING WORKED UPON. REMEMBER TO MAKE TIP AND TEMPERATURE ADJUSTMENTS WHEN NECESSARY IN ORDER TO ACHIEVE THE DESIRED EFFECTS.

Combining Textures

Combining various textures offers even more variety. There is one basic thing to remember when combining textures: YOU SHOULD USUALLY WORK WITH ONE BASICALLY FLAT TEXTURE FOR THE BACKGROUND AND ONE RAISED TEXURE FOR ACCENT.

A hammered background can be beautifuley accented with a row of shells, scallops or pearls. The soft, flat appearance of the hammered surface adds a very effective background for the high, shiny appearance of scallops, pearls and shells (see Fig. 5-I).

FIG. 5-I....Combining Hammered Background With Various Other Textures

When cleaned, patined and polished the effect of combined textures is quite spectacular. We frequently use texture combinations like these on jewelry boxes and terrariums. Insignificant seams can be decorated with a hammered texture. Important seams in the lid may first be hammered and then accented with scallops. This method of lid decoration makes it possible to achieve an elegant affect from the simplest of designs. You may find that you no longer need to have lids of 10 or 20 pieces. Simple elegance is a desired quality in stained glass (see Fig. 5-J).

FIG. 5-J....Quick And Easy Jewelry Box Lid

Another simple, yet effective, combination is to hammer the basic bead and apply alternating, evenly spaced, bamboo globs (see Fig. 5-K).

FIG. 5-K....Combining Hammered With Bamboo

This creates a high-low, high-low, or polished-dull, polished-dull, effect. This combination is quite effective on a masculine project, where you don't want to get too cute.

These combinations are best used on geometric structures or in borders. The effect is quite subtle. They do not detract from the structure or subject matter of the window.

REMEMBER TO BE CAREFUL NOT TO OVERTEXTURE YOUR WORK—IT CAN DETRACT FROM YOUR PIECE IF OVERDONE. YOU WANT TO USE TEXTURING TO ENHANCE YOUR WORK, NOT OVERPOWER IT.

Clean - Patina - Wash 6

The final step in your project is the cleaning, patining, and polishing. This sometimes becomes a problem on projects that are textured very heavily. In areas with exaggerated highs and lows, it is often quite difficult to thoroughly clean the lows and crevices between higher textures. These areas seldom can be polished to a bright sheen.

Having brightly polished highs and dull dark backgrounds is not necessarily undesirable, though. That is what often makes the texture "jump out" at you. When planning what texture to use on your project take these highs and lows into consideration. Plan which areas you want to appear as a darker background. Plan the highly polished areas to be around the focal points on your piece (see Fig. 6-A).

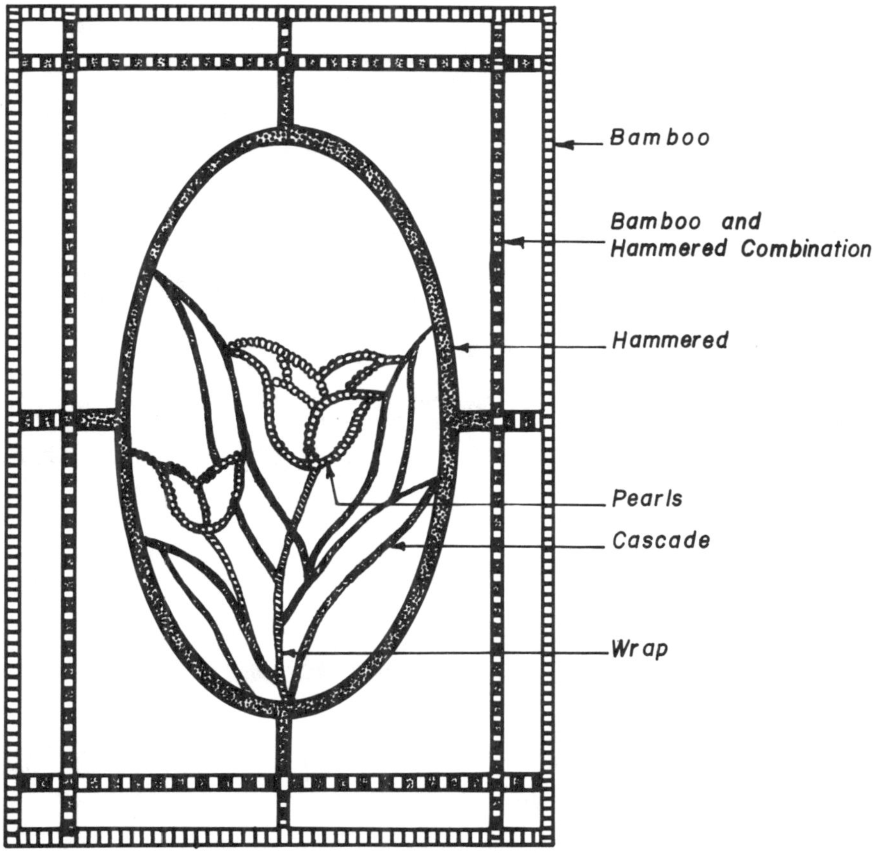

FIG. 6-A....Use Of Textures On A Window

Some craftspersons who have been working with this technique in creating jewelry, have been having their pieces gold electroplated. If you would like to have this done consult a jeweler or someone at a lapidary supply store. They can put you in touch with someone who can do the process. There are some special procedures that must be followed prior to electroplating. Primarily, the object must be VERY clean. It must be free of all chemicals commonly used in soldering. You may use them in creating your piece, but they must be THOROUGHLY REMOVED prior to electroplating.

If you are not going to electroplate you basically proceed with finishing as you would on any other soldered project. You must take care to treat all areas, high and low.

1. THOROUGHLY RINSE the project in warm water. If there are a lot of deep crevices or gaps you must scrub those areas with a stiff bristled brush (a toothbrush works well) while holding it under warm rinse water. We do not recommend using wire bristles. Scrubbing the entire project is actually a good idea to ensure that it is completely clean. Do not use soap at this point as it can contaminate the areas to be patined.

2. The object should then be briskly buffed dry with a clean terry cloth towel. This will polish the high areas. Be sure to thoroughly dry the lows, too.

3. Apply patina with a cloth. If low areas cannot be reached you may have to use a brush. When all areas have been treated rinse under warm water to remove excess patina.

4. The piece may now be THOROUGHLY washed with a mild soap. Some light scrubbing might again be necessary; this might, however, remove some patina from the high areas.

5. Thoroughly dry with a terry cloth towel. Rubbing briskly, but lightly, will begin to polish the high areas. If this gives you the desired effect you are done. If you desire a more polished look proceed with Step 6.

6. Your stained glass dealer will recommend a polish that is suitable for polishing patina. Apply the polish with your fingertip to the areas you desire to polish. The use of a cloth can result in the patina being rubbed off. The polish

can be buffed off with a clean, dry terry cloth towel. DO NOT RUB TOO HARD OR TOO LONG, as this can remove patina. Any polish that has dried in the low areas must be washed out or corrosion will occur in the future.

THE PIECE MAY NOW BE MAINTAINED BY CLEANING WITH A GOOD PROFESSIONAL (AMMONIA-FREE) GLASS CLEANER.

If you do not wish to patina your project you should follow the above procedures, omitting the use of the patina. You may experiment using an electric polishing tool if you wish. We recommend using a very lightweight (low abrasive) polish if a power tool is used. Once again you must thoroughly clean the piece after polishing has been completed to prevent corrosion from any chemicals remaining from the polish.

7 Special Projects

This type of DECORATIVE SOLDERING is not exclusively useful in traditional stained glass. Many of us have begun to experiment with jewelry, belt buckles, and free-form structures. Sometimes it is fun, and quite rewarding, to break from your usual projects and play a little. It offers a chance to be very innovative and expressive.

Sculpture

Most of us are collectors of miscellaneous junk. It is amazing what can be created with a few shells, a piece of driftwood, polished stones, feathers, glass globs, small scraps of glass, sheet metal (copper or brass), etc. If you can foil it or wrap it with copper wire, you can cluster it and add a little decorative soldering to create a beautiful free-form sculpture. If you have a few shells, foil them and arrange them on a piece of driftwood. Add some wire or foil to the areas of the driftwood where you want to add the shells. Position the shells on the driftwood and solder them in place. Add complimentary texturing (i.e., shells, pearls and/or hammered) to the foiled areas (see Fig. 7-A).

FIG. 7-A....Sculpture Of Found Objects And Various Textures

On areas that are difficult to foil you may have to drill and attach with copper wire. These wires can be secured with solder and textured. Scrap sheet copper or brass can be cut with shears and bent into the shape of a seagull in flight. This may be attached to a piece of metal rod, textured, and attached to the arrangement (see Fig. 7-B).

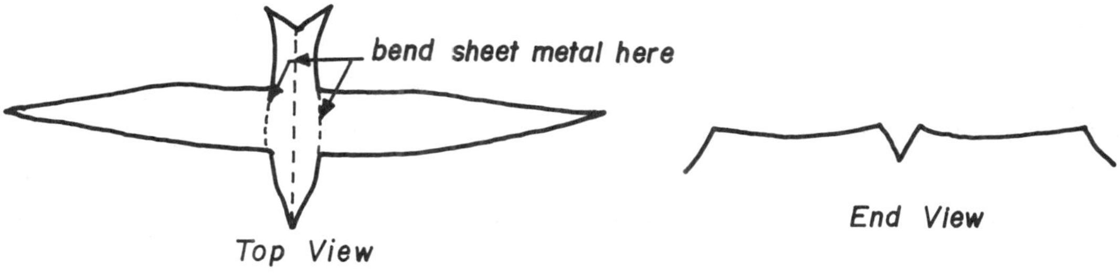

FIG. 7-B....Sheet Metal Seagull

Polished stones may be wrapped with thin foil or copper wire and attached together in a cluster. This, in turn, may be attached to a piece of wood or a larger stone. Additional foil may be added to give areas upon which to texture. A few decorative feathers may be stuck between the smaller stones for variety. Feathers should be added after the object has been washed, patined, and polished (see Fig. 7-C).

FIG. 7-C....Sculpture Of Polished Stones And Feathers

Belt Buckles

A great way to show off your new soldering technique is on belt buckles. There are basically two types that can be made: stained glass and lapidary (polished stone). The first thing to concern yourself with is the belt buckle hardware itself. This can pose a problem, but there are many possible solutions. For optimum strength you will need a solid surface to work on; neither thin slab stone nor glass are strong enough to be used alone.

Basically you want to work with something that is no smaller than 1-1/2" by 3" for women and 2" by 3-1/2" for men. Either oval or rectangular shapes work well. The easy way is to find an old, flat-surfaced belt buckle around the house. If none are available try garage sales, thrift shops, hobby shops, lapidary or leather supply shops. Often you can find a blank brass or copper buckle designed for decorating. Try not to buy a heavy, thick buckle blank, as you will be adding quite a bit of additional weight. Copper or brass is ideal because you can solder directly on them. If you find aluminum or some other solder-resistant metal you can always wrap the entire buckle with copper foil. This is a little more work but often is the most economical method. The buckle should be as flat as possible, but a little curve will not hurt.

Most buckle blanks come with hardware attached. Some require attaching the loop and tab. Be sure to ask for instructions on attaching these when you purchase them. Positioning is important.

Once you have your buckle you must determine how to decorate it. You may make a small stained glass panel to cover the entire surface of the blank buckle. Use small pieces so that you can form them over the curve of the buckle blank (see Fig. 7-D).

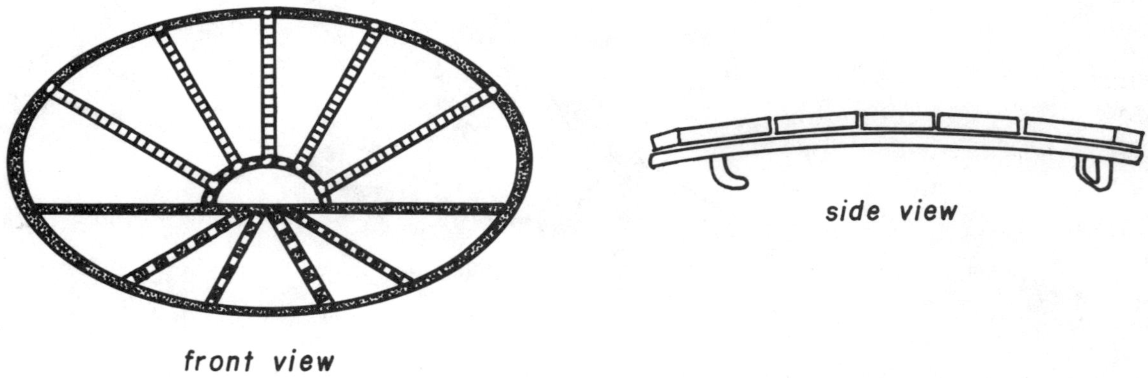

FIG. 7-D....Stained Glass Belt Buckle - Whole Scene

You will have some pieces of glass, depending on their size and position, which may sit up above the buckle surface. A good heavy application of your solder technique should offer the glass adequate support and protection. The glass used should be opalescent, as no light will pass through it. You may leave some backgrounds open (see Fig. 7-E). These can be filled with solder and textured.

FIG. 7-E....Stained Glass Belt Buckles - Textured Solder Background

Soldering should be built up from the edges to completely protect the edges of the glass pieces (see Fig. 7-E). A good finishing touch is to solder the back of the buckle, too. This is a necessary step if you foil wrapped the buckle blank before soldering. Patina, wash, and polish following the instructions in Chapter 6.

The second style of buckle uses polished stones. Small pieces of slab agate work well. These are available from lapidary supply stores. Some large hobby stores may also stock them. You may use one large stone or a cluster of small ones.

Fig. 7-F shows some typical arrangements and positioning. Cut and polished stones are beautiful and come in all shapes, sizes, and colors. They look beautiful when framed with decorative soldering. The stones should not exceed 1/8" in thickness. You can foil them just as you would a piece of glass. When you have foiled them, arrange them on the blank buckle and tack them in place. Try not to position them too close to the edges, to prevent possible damage to them in the future.

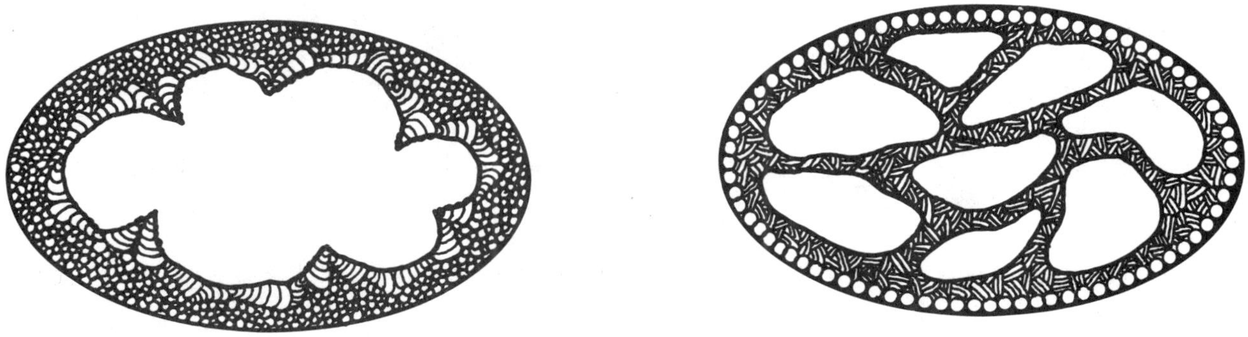

FIG. 7-F....Belt Buckles - Polished Stones And Textured Solder

Again you must build up a good solder bead around them to protect them as stones are no stronger than glass. Add decorative textures to the solder. Finishing by patining, washing, and polishing as described in Chapter 6.

Jewelry

While you are in the lapidary supply store, keep your eye out for a few polished stones (they don't have to be slab type) that might make pretty jewelry. Keep in mind that you will have to mount them some way, either by foil wrapping the edge or making a couple of wraps around them with wire. You may want to select stones that have interesting or irregular grooves in them that might provide a space to wrap. Fig. 7-G, shows some interesting effects achieved with foil and wire wraps around stones.

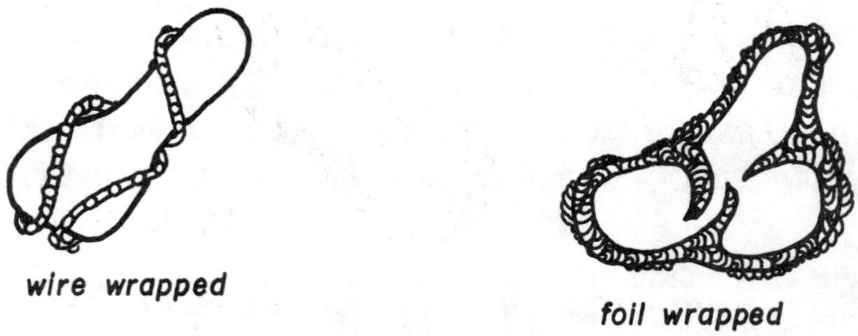

FIG. 7-G....Wrapping Polished Stones

A loop can be added at the top at which to attach a chain or cord (see Fig. 7-G). This loop must be firmly soldered into place. Long wire legs, extending from the loop, should be concealed under decorative soldering (see Fig. 7-H).

FIG. 7-H....Adding Wire Loops To Wrapped Stones

The soldering required in this project must be delicate and should complement the piece. The delicate work requires the use of a small tip, cool iron, and solder with a high tin content. Working on small areas and narrow edges requires great patience and finesse. Your iron must be set at a low temperature, as the areas superheat very quickly, causing rapid meltdowns of your texturing. Shells and pearls in conjunction with hammered surfaces are very effective in jewelry.

Lovely jewelry sets can be made using large stones for a necklace and small, matching stones for drop earings. Larger stones, too large for jewelry, can be made into key chains in the same manner (see Fig. 7-I).

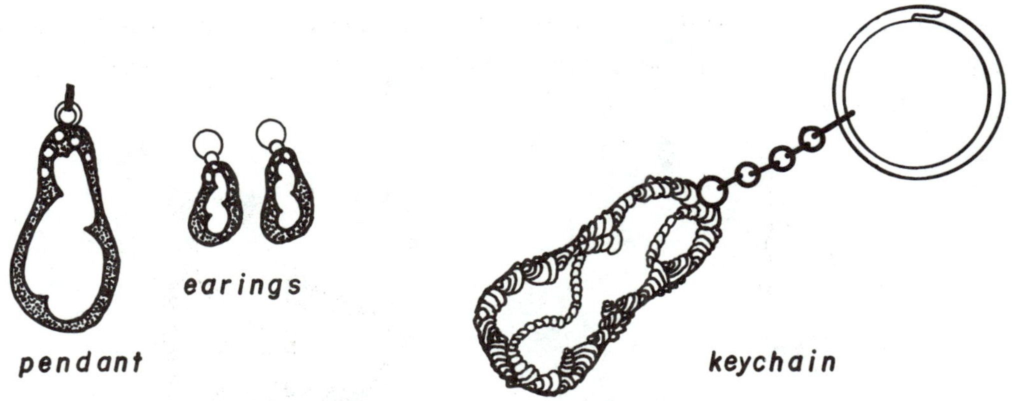

FIG. 7-I....Some Projects For Polished Stones And Decorative Solder

Shells can be made into jewelry in the same manner. Some shells even have a natural hole in them through which you can easily attach the wire loop (see Fig. 7-J).

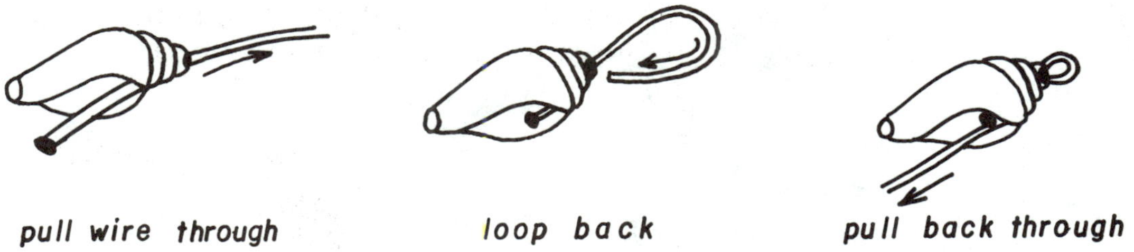

FIG. 7-J....Adding A Wire Loop To Shells With A Hole

You might consider clustering a few shells together and connecting them with very delicate beadwork over wire (see Fig. 7-K).

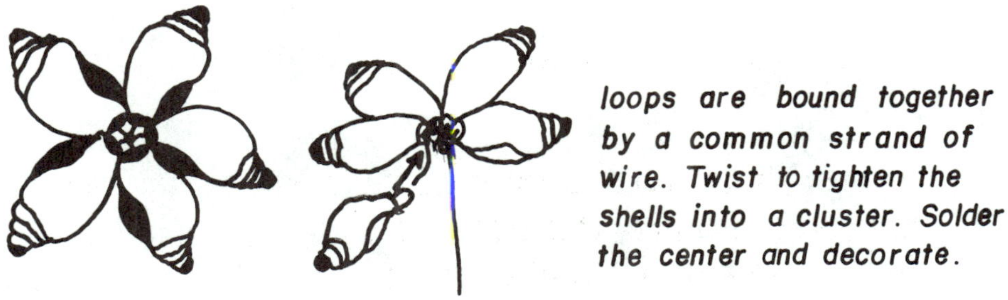

FIG. 7-K....Flowers Made From Shells

Larger necklaces can be made by using a large shell, from which you can hang a cluster or clusters of staggered shells (see Fig. 7-L).

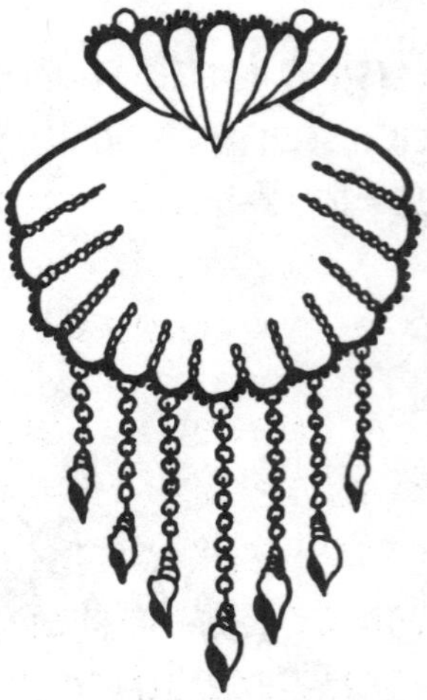

FIG. 7-L....Large Shell Necklace

Lapidary and hobby stores also handle jewelry findings upon which you can mount stones or shells to create a beautiful pin. You can glue the pre-decorated stones to the findings with a good epoxy glue. Ask a salesperson at the hobby store for a recommendation (see Fig. 7-M).

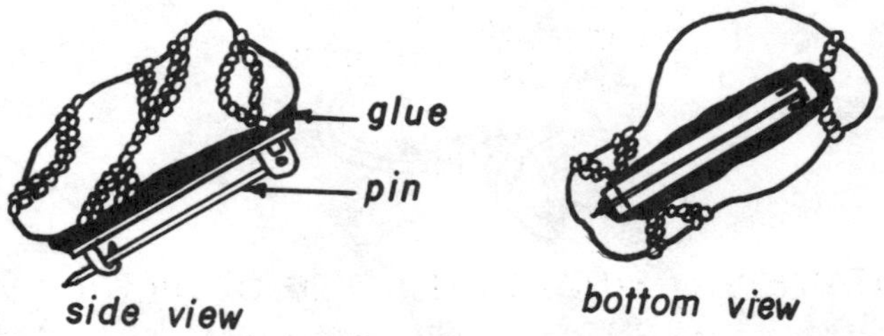

FIG. 7-M....Attaching Jewelry Findings With Glue

If you do not wish to glue the decorated object you may wrap the stone or shell in such a manner as to provide a place at which to solder the finding to the stone or shell (see Fig. 7-N).

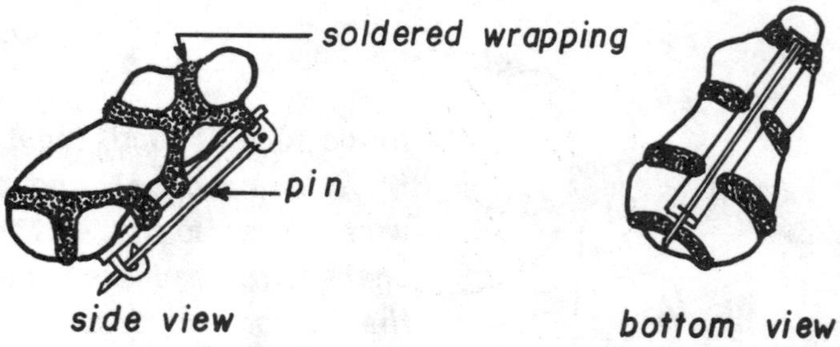

FIG. 7-N....Attaching Jewelry Findings With Solder

REMEMBER TO USE AS LITTLE SOLDER AS POSSIBLE WHEN DECORATING A PIN, AS EXCESSIVE WEIGHT WILL CAUSE THE PIN TO HANG POORLY.

Decorative Objects

Another way to use your new soldering technique is to decorate pre-made objects. By "pre-made" objects, I mean vases, goblets, flower pots, urns, lamp bases, etc. Basically almost anything can be decorated with solder.

The entire object can be covered or just certain areas. The object need not be made of metal, either. If it isn't made of solderable metal you can cover it with copper foil. Copper foil is available in narrow strips or in sheet form. The sheet foil is best used on large flat areas. It either can be covered entirely, or areas of foil can be cut out for open spaces or to allow what is beneath to show through (see Fig. 7-O).

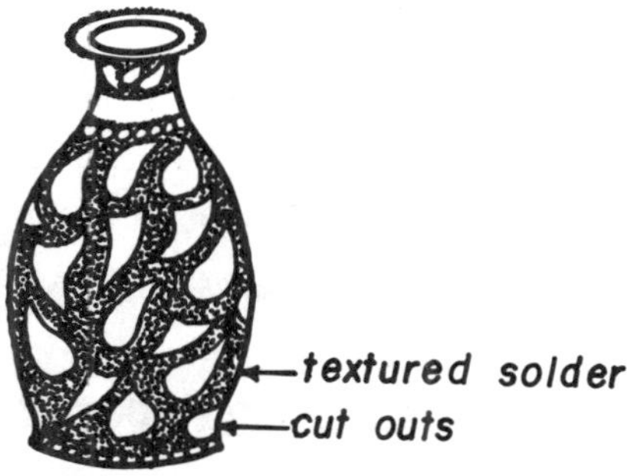

FIG. 7-O....Trimming Foil To Create Voids

If the object that you are working on is made of metal, which might be affected by solder, you might mask it off with masking tape. This will keep the masked area from being soldered upon. This is very effective when working on a brass object (see Fig. 7-P).

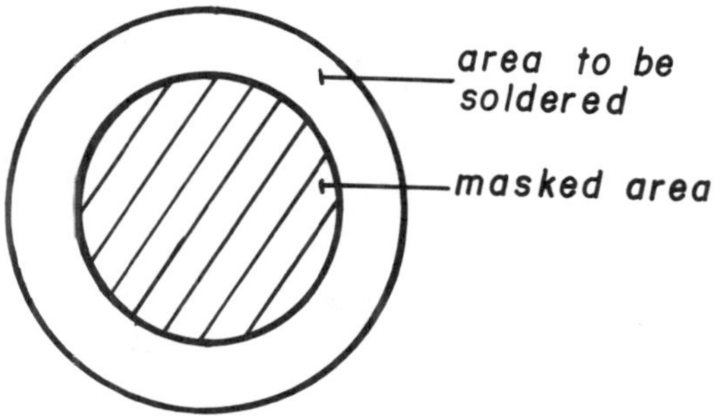

FIG. 7-P....Masking To Prevent Soldering

Small pieces of polished stone, glass, or glass globs can be foiled and attached to add contrast or decoration. Decorative soldering is then applied around them and to the other areas of the object that you wish to decorate (see Fig. 7-Q).

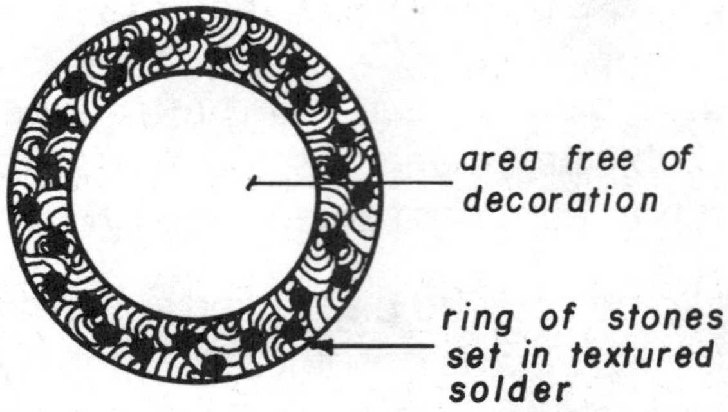

FIG. 7-Q....Decorated Plates

Many unusual and inexpensive objects can be purchased at discount and import stores. These objects can serve as a base for decorative soldering. Many of these things are made of brass or copper, which makes your preparation very easy. Sometimes you must buff them with very fine steel wool to remove their protective coating. Once you have done this you need only flux and solder. Remember that you can mask certain areas to keep areas of brass showing on the finished product.

Use a 1/4" tip on full heat for the initial coat of solder as much of the heat will be absorbed by the object itself, until the object heats up. Once the object has heated, you may be able to switch to a smaller tip or reduce the heat to achieve the desired textures. This will vary greatly from object to object. Some very large pieces may have to be worked entirely with a 1/4" tip.

I recently purchased a set of small, inexpensive ($6.00) brass candlesticks and a brass goblet ($4.50) at a local import store. By adding a few glass globs and masking certain areas I was able to create a set that looks like it came from King Arthur's

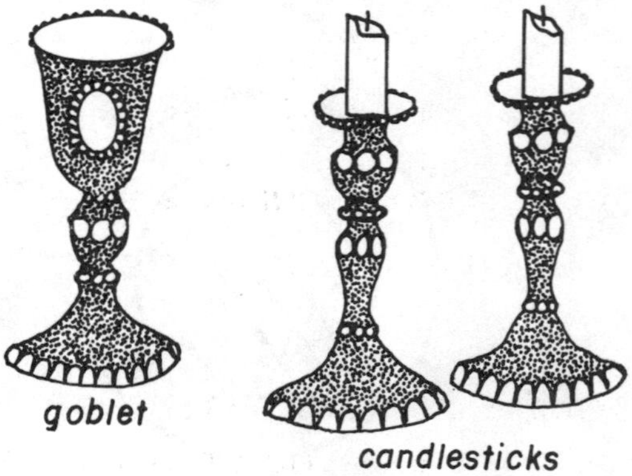

FIG. 7-R....A Decoratve Set

table. I decorated them with flat shells, pearls and scallops. The entire project took only four hours (see Fig. 7-R).

If glass is used as the base structure for your decorative work, be advised that it may crack with the amount of heat used in decorating the object. This need not pose a problem if no glass is visible on the project. You should foil and solder the inner surfaces that will be visible when the project is finished.

If you wish to use the object as a vase, that will need to hold water, you must seal the finished project to prevent leakage. This can be done by melting ordinary wax and coating the entire inside surface of the project. You may brush it on or pour some into the vase and rotate it so that the wax coats all inside surfaces. You will have to be careful in the future not to scrape the wax off and possibly cause a leak. Using resin is also an excellent and more durable method of sealing a vase.

A great way to make a lamp base to match a shade that you have made, or would like to make, is to use this new soldering technique. Go to a local dime store, hardware store or thrift shop and find a lamp base that is basically the size and shape that you want. The material it is made of is not important (plastic, however, should not be used). Remove the wiring, as it may melt during decorating, and foil the areas that you wish to decorate. Remember that areas of polished brass or cut glass will provide beautiful accents. You may also want to leave cut-out areas if you are working on a ceramic base (see Fig. 7-S).

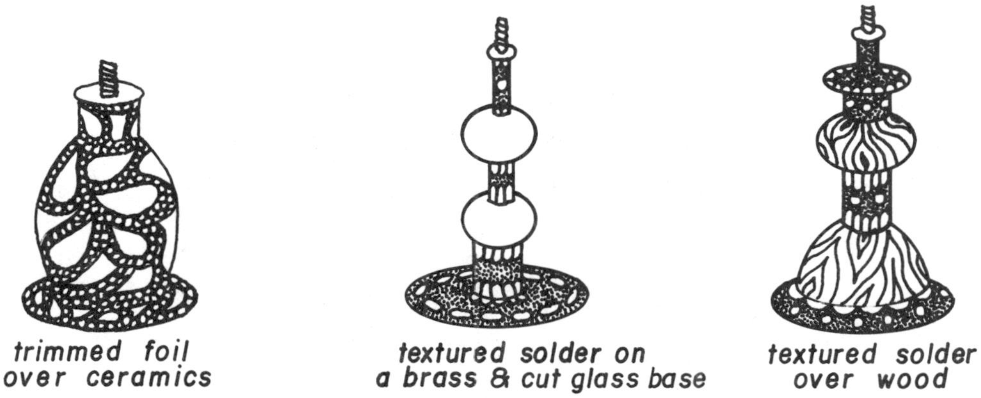

FIG. 7-S....Lamp Bases

You may add accents of the glass that was used in the lampshade for a lovely coordinated appearance. Use the same decorative textures that you used on the shade. The added weight of the solder should make even the lighest base heavy enough to support a Tiffany-style shade. If not, consult a lighting store about adding additional weight.

When the base has been patined, washed, and polished the wiring may be reinstalled.

THESE HAVE BEEN JUST A FEW SUGGESTIONS OF UNUSUAL WAYS TO APPLY YOUR NEW SOLDERING TECHNIQUE. THEY OFFER YOU A WAY TO DIVERSIFY YOUR LINE IF YOU ARE A PROFESSIONAL, OR EXPAND YOUR CREATIVITY IF YOU ARE A HOBBYIST.

8 Finishing Touches using Decorative Soldering

One real advantage of knowing decorative soldering is that you can easily decorate and conceal wire hangers for small window panels and terrariums. Legs and knobs can be made and SECURELY attached to a jewelry box and decorated.

These additions are not only functional but add a beautiful finishing touch to your piece. Small window panels can have decorative wire hangers made that can be secured into the surrounding framework (see Fig. 8-A).

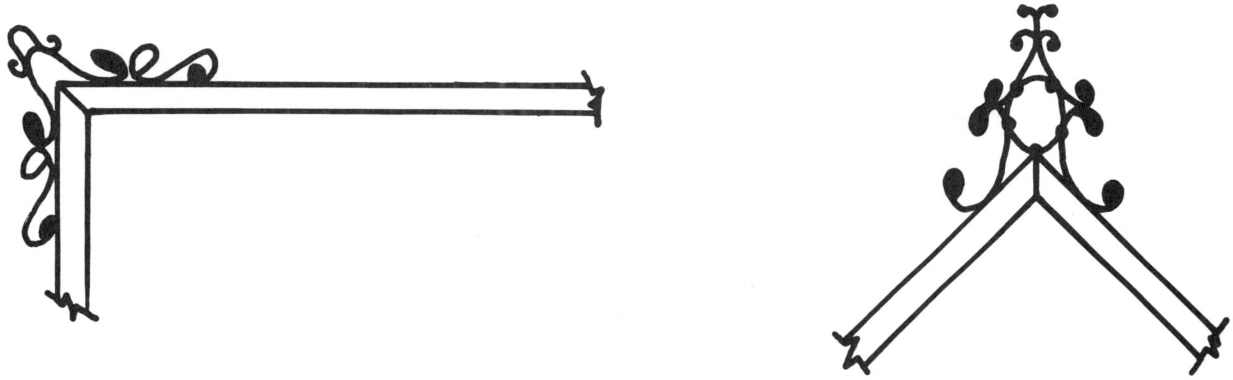

FIG. 8-A....Hanging Loops For Small Window Panels

Jewelry boxes can have legs made of bent wire that is decorated and secured to the corners of the box. You can make knobs to match (see Fig. 8-B).

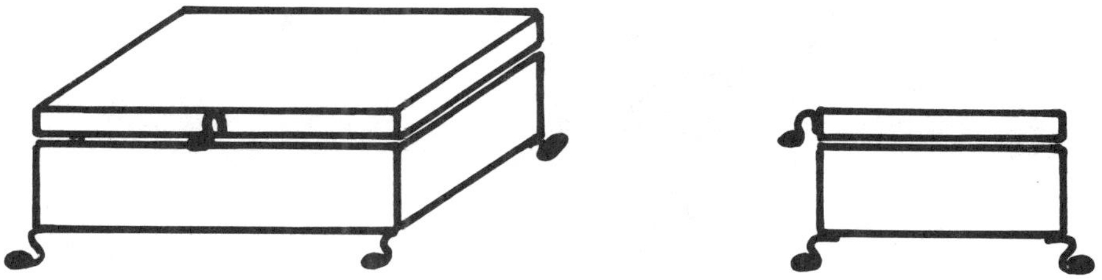

FIG. 8-B....Matching Knob And Legs

To hang a terrarium you can make an elaborate loop that is both functional and decorative. They may be secured into the panels of the terrarium. Decorative soldering will conceal any reinforcements (see Fig. 8-C).

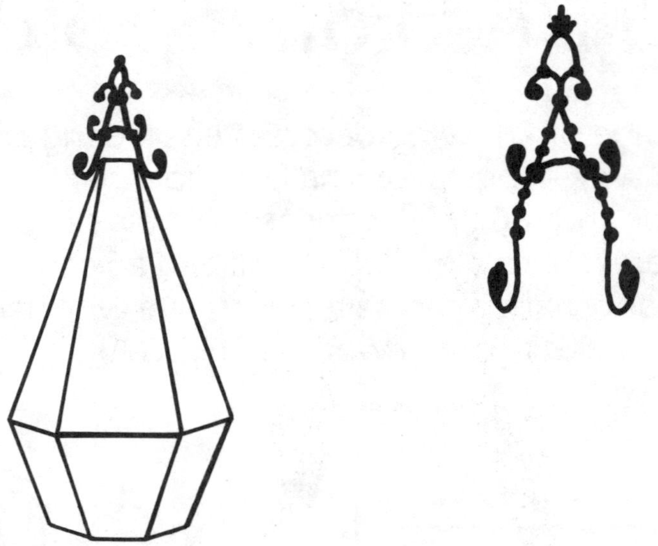

FIG. 8-C....Terrarium Hanging Loops

Shapes should be bent from pieces of brass rod or heavy copper wire, using needle nose pliers. For consistent curves you can bend the wire around something small and round, oval, or square. These shapes can be coated with solder. Additional decorative shapes can be soldered onto the primary shape to give it a more lacy appearance. Small loops can be filled in to give the shape more mass (see Fig. 8-D).

FIG. 8-D....Wire Loop Assemblies

The primary hanging portion of the loop should be securely attached to your work at at least two points. Small decorative loops can be attached around the primary loop, but care should be taken not to hang the object from these appendages—they are for decorative purposes only. The entire loop or loop construction should be solder-coated to maintain consistency of appearance. Small loops can be filled in and textured. Pearls can be added to any of the solder-coated wire for additional decoration. See Fig. 8-E for a typical hanging loop.

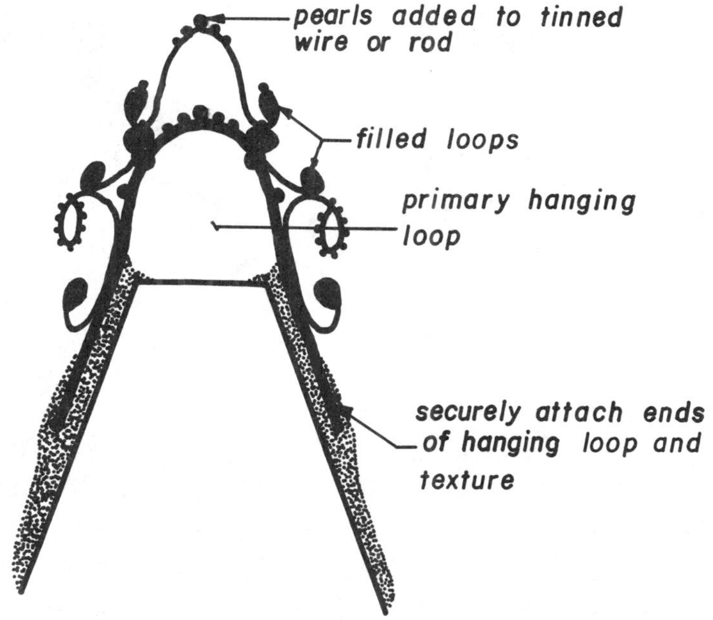

FIG. 8-E....Detail Of Hanging Loop

If your pieces are to be applied in pairs be sure to make the two loops of consistent size and shape. This is most easily done by forming your loops around something. Two wires bent around the same piece of wood dowel will form two loops of the same size and shape.

To make simple "S" shapes you can use brass "Jack Chain" and twist it flat. One or both end loops can be bent open to give the desired shape (see Fig. 8-F).

FIG. 8-F....Creating With Chain Links

These separated and altered links of chain can be spaced around a small panel to give a decorative border (see Fig. 8-G). Be sure to solder-coat the links before attaching them to your piece or to each other.

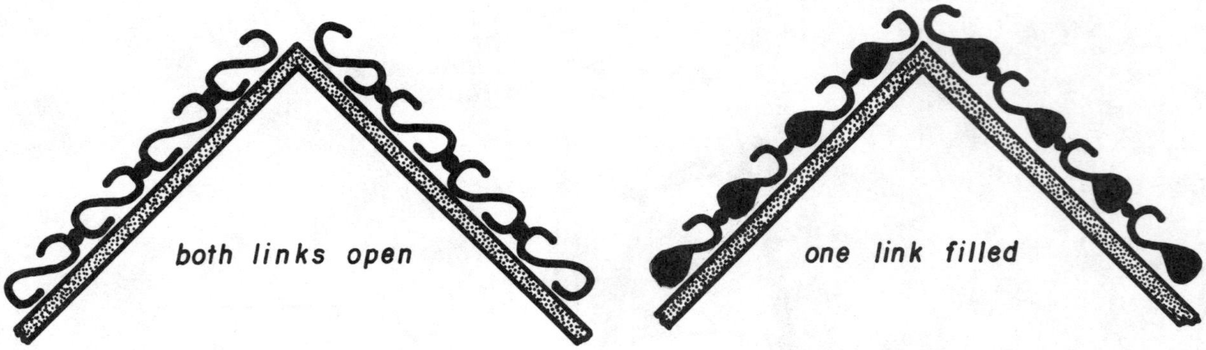

FIG. 8-G....Decorative Borders Made With Chain Links

Lift knobs and legs for boxes can be easily formed by bending jack chain links, too. One closed loop can be bent to form the pad of the leg. The other loop can be opened and straightened so that it may be soldered into the bottom seam of the box. All surfaces must be solder-coated. The bottom loop foot can be filled in and textured. Fig. 8-H shows a leg made from a bent chain loop and how to attach it.

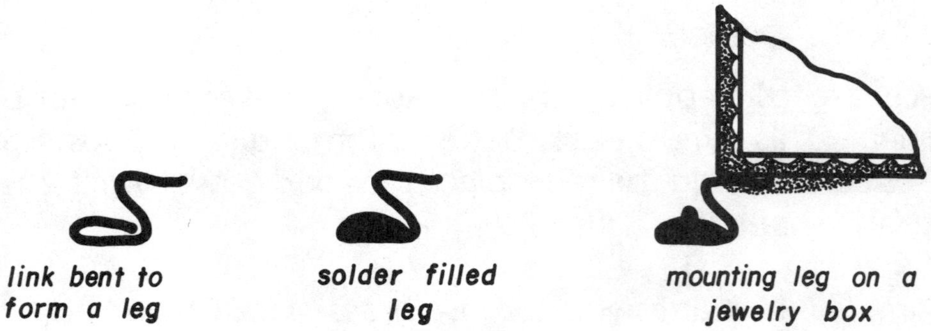

FIG. 8-H....Legs Made From Chain Links

A matching lift knob can be made by similarly bending the chain, but the straightened loop must be bent for easy attachment to the box lid. You may trim the straight leg slightly to aid in attachment. Again, solder-coat the surface and texture, if desired. Fig. 8-I shows a typical lift knob and typical methods of attachment.

FIG. 8-I....Knobs Made From Chain Links

You can also purchase, from a hobby store, precut copper shapes which can be solder-coated and decorated and used as lift knobs on boxes (see Fig. 8-J).

FIG. 8-J....Common Shapes Of Precut Copper

If your hobby store does not carry these shapes you can make them by cutting any desired shape from heavy copper or brass sheet, using metal shears.

Coat the shape heavily with solder, front and back. Attach the knob to the box before texturing. Try to plan your texture pattern to include heavy reinforcement at points of attachment (see Fig. 8-K). Remember that box lids are often heavy, and the knob should be securely soldered onto the edge of the box lid.

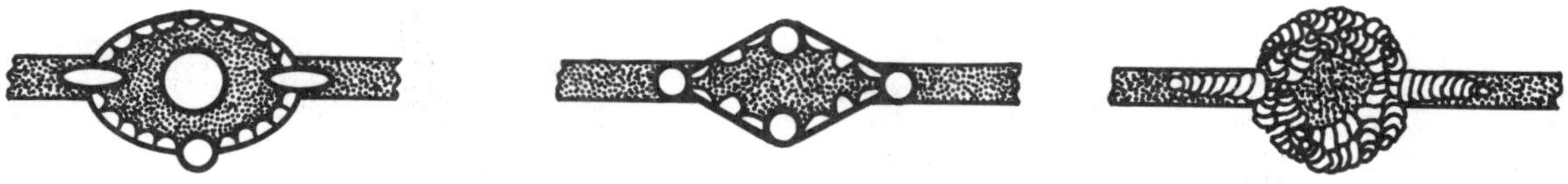

FIG. 8-K....Mounting Decorated Knobs To Lids

The most important thing to remember when making hanging loops or knobs is to make them secure. When designing them keep in mind how and at what points you are going to attach them.

Wire hangers must be made of a material strong enough to support the weight of the piece. Remember to hang the piece from the primary loop only. Decorative, secondary loops are not strong enough to hang the object from.

Legs must be strong enough to support the weight of the box. They should be bent evenly to ensure that the box rests evenly on a flat surface. The pads of a leg should be of sufficient mass to prevent marring of the surface they rest on.

Decorative soldering enables you to conceal any reinforcing solder that you must apply to attach something securely—SO BE SURE TO ADD AS MUCH SOLDER AS NECESSARY!

You have just read about a new technique that will enable you to greatly enhance your craftsmenship. You will now be able to add distinctive accents to your projects. No project is too large or small to be decorated with this new technique.

We have taught you the basics. With the knowledge from this book you can combine textures or create your own. Experiment, that is the key to creativity.